A Survival Kit for Harassed Parents

★ Suggestions for an individual child or a group of children.
★ *Games a child can play alone are starred.*
★ Special chapters on science experiments, nature projects, dramatics, music, reading, and developing hobbies.
★ Hundreds of jokes, riddles, and tongue twisters.
★ Delicious recipes for easy-to-make candy.
★ All the activities carefully selected so as not to make too much noise or create a mess.
★ Every idea *child-tested* for interest, facility, and fun!

"When cries of there's nothing to do arise on the next rainy day, the wise parent will have on hand a copy of this book. The author has brought together enough play ideas to keep children busy for a month of rainy days!"
—*Library Journal*

"This book has many uses for sunny days, too, and as a source book for birthday party games and vacation fun."
—*Los Angeles Times*

The Rainy Day Book
was originally published by
Trident Press.

Also by Alvin Schwartz

How to Fly a Kite, Catch a Fish, Grow a Flower

Published by Pocket Books

The Rainy Day Book

by
Alvin Schwartz

A POCKET BOOK EDITION published by
Simon & Schuster of Canada, Ltd. • Richmond Hill, Ontario, Canada
Registered User of the Trademark

THE RAINY DAY BOOK

Trident Press edition published May, 1968

A *Pocket Book* edition
1st printing...........August, 1969
2nd printing...........August, 1969

This *Pocket Book* edition includes every word
contained in the original, higher-priced edition. It is printed from
brand-new plates made from completely reset, clear, easy-to-read type.
Trademarks registered in the United States and other countries.
Standard Book Number: 671-75452-1.
Library of Congress Catalog Card Number: 68-14288.

Copyright, ©, 1968, by Alvin Schwartz. All rights reserved.

Printed in Canada

For Nancy and Betsy

ACKNOWLEDGMENTS

SOME OF THE ACTIVITIES *described in this book were hastily devised in moments of stress. However, most were brought home by our children, suggested by other parents or by recreation experts, or inspired by various books on specialized aspects of recreation.*

For the ideas they contributed I am grateful to my children: John, twelve, Peter, ten, Nancy, nine, and Elizabeth, seven; to my wife Barbara; to members of the staff of the National Recreation and Park Association, who have been of unfailing assistance in all my writing on recreation; to the children's librarians at the New York Public Library and the libraries in Princeton and Trenton, N. J.; to Ellin Greene, former Storytelling Specialist at the New York Public Library; to Anne Voss of the New Jersey State Library and members of her staff; to Eleanor VanVechten of Riverside School, Princeton, N. J.; to Rachele Thomas of the Child Study Association of America; and to many friends and neighbors.

I wish to thank Redbook Magazine, *the* Chicago Tribune–New York Daily News Syndicate, *and* Parents' Magazine *for permission to reprint material I originally prepared for them. I also thank James Dickey,* The New York Times Book Review, This Week Magazine, *and* Pocket Books *for permitting me to reprint copyrighted materials.*

Alvin Schwartz

Contents

Rain on the Roof — 11

1. **QUIET GAMES** — 15
   Relatively noiseless activities that require a minimum of physical activity and make use of easily found, everyday materials . . . very practical when space is limited.

2. **ARTS AND CRAFTS** — 51
   All kinds of things to make or remake . . . toys, decorations, gifts, clothing, masks, jewelry, puzzles . . . useful projects for children of all ages.

3. **DRAMATIC PLAY** — 82
   Housebound children can discover the fun of being actor, producer, or puppeteer on their own make-believe stage . . . beginner's tips on costumery, makeup, puppets and dolls, props, lighting effects.

4. **WATER PLAY** — 96
   An inexpensive and clean source of wet fun for everyone . . . from bubbles and bubble games to indoor fishing, sailing, and bathing.

5. **ATTICS, BASEMENTS, CLOSETS, DRAWERS** — 100
   Ideas on the amazing treasures to be found in every home . . . youthful nostalgia and hours of discovery and amusement among old clothes, dusty boxes, and other forgotten things.

8 / THE RAINY DAY BOOK

6. HOBBIES 102
   The fun of collecting things—from autographs and buttons to keys and stamps ... scrapbook ideas and clues to related hobbies.

7. KEEPING DIARIES, WRITING LETTERS 108
   Secret sources of much private pleasure ... ideas for corresponding with pen pals around the world.

8. NATURE 110
   Exploring the living world in and around the house ... how to make an indoor garden, examine flowers, force buds to bloom, preserve leaves, collect indoor insects.

9. SCIENCE EXPERIMENTS 118
   Simple and safe scientific projects for kids who would appreciate the mystery behind bouncing buttons, a bone that bends, and thread that dances.

10. PUZZLES 125
    Checker and cut-out puzzles that have challenged children for 4,000 years ... also codes and secret writing techniques.

11. JOKES, RIDDLES, TONGUE TWISTERS 136
    Funny, silly, sometimes ridiculous stories ... crazy questions that defy explanation ... and rhymes that will twist every tongue.

12. MUSIC 146
    Suggestions for developing interest in music ... ideas for making simple instruments ... sources of song material.

13. STORYTELLING 152
    An introduction to the pleasures and wonders of storytelling ... lists of books suitable for every age level.

14. GOOD THINGS TO EAT   161
    Fun in the kitchen with delicious easy to make recipes . . . from popcorn balls and peanut brittle to somemores and taffy.

15. LETTING OFF STEAM   168
    Active games for restless children . . . some noisy activities . . . from Balloon Ball to Simon says . . . healthful (energy using) exercises and helpful household chores.

16. EXCURSIONS IN THE RAIN   176
    Aquariums, firehouses, libraries, museums, shops, the weather bureau, and other places to explore when all else fails.

17. SOLUTIONS TO PUZZLES   178

    Index   183

We carry within us the wonders we seek without us....

                                        Sir Thomas Browne

Rain on the Roof

WHEN AN ARTICLE I wrote on recreation for housebound children appeared a few years ago in one of the women's magazines, it was accompanied by a cartoon which showed three young children in Indian headdresses in a rainy day activity with their mother. Two of the children leaped about shrieking much as real Indians might have done before going on the warpath. The third worked busily at tying Mother into a chair. He already had bound her legs and gagged her mouth. Now, smirking evilly, he lashed her arms in place.

What the cartoonist was saying, of course, is that the only way to keep things under control on a rainy day is by keeping your children under control, and that the way to do this is by keeping them occupied. Otherwise, who knows what might happen? It was the standard message, but it wasn't quite what I had in mind.

Sooner or later on a rainy day most children do run out of ideas and need help in finding new activities. But of more consequence than how many games a mother knows or how creative she is with empty oatmeal containers is how she approaches the situation to begin with.

Few mothers I have met yearn for a rainy day. Many I have talked to see such a day as an exhausting obstacle course in which they not only must keep their children under control but also must do their housekeeping. Under the circumstances it might be wise to forget some of the housework and try for a more leisurely, flexible day.

Certainly one of the potential pleasures of a rainy day is getting to know your child a little better, not only helping him at play but sharing household tasks with him, listening to music and reading together, or simply sitting around and talking—experiences for which there may be no opportunity when the weather is fair and a youngster is free to play outdoors.

Another of the pleasures of such a day is perhaps more selfish, but no less desirable. It is the chance to do what you like best, if only for a short while, or to explore those interests for which you may be too busy at other times.

One mother I know abandons her usual routine on a day she and her two children spend indoors. She cooks and cleans only enough to get by. Then she sews or reads or serves as companion to them according to her mood and theirs. Everyone doesn't always have a good time. But it certainly is worth the attempt. Making the most of a rainy day is far more important than making the beds and washing the kitchen floor. Usually it also is more fun.

ACTIVITIES AND MATERIALS

As in all human endeavor, the games, crafts, puzzles, and other activities in this book are based on skill, chance, exploration, experimentation, or silliness. I was introduced to many of these activities as a child. You probably will find that this was your experience too. In fact, some of the games and puzzles suggested have been in use throughout the world for hundreds, even thousands of years.

Most of what is needed in the way of materials and equipment is likely to be found in any household. In line with this, the activities in the chapters "Quiet Games" and "Arts and Crafts" are organized in terms of the materials needed. Using this system you can determine quickly what is feasible and what is not. If you have a balloon, for example, you will find three games in which it can be used. If you have a shoebox there are at least a half-dozen ways to put it to use. On the other hand, if you are seeking a particular game or project, consult the Index.

A star (*) in front of an activity indicates that it is suitable for one or more children. In a number of cases the designation is used with a game that traditionally has required two participants but can be modified easily for use by one. My son Peter, for example, greatly enjoys playing the card game War by himself. He does this by pitting his left hand against his right hand. He, of course, is completely neutral. In chapters where all the activities are suitable for one child the star is not used.

Almost a thousand possibilities for fun are described. However, the objective is not to provide all the activities with which to fill a child's day, but rather to offer ideas and points of departure. Your youngster is likely to have projects of his own he'd like to pursue. There also may be times when he prefers to do absolutely nothing. As every grownup can appreciate, this can often be just as pleasant as keeping busy.

ALVIN SCHWARTZ

1 ❈ Quiet Games

GAMES USING:

Balloons	Drinking Straws	Paper and Pencil
Balls	Fruit	Paper Plates
Beans	Herbs and Spices	Peppercorns
Books	Identification	Playing Cards
Boxes	Kitchen Timers	Questions
Buttons and Counters	Laughter	Searches
Calendars	Magazines	Thread
Candy	Marbles	Thread Spools
Checkers	Memory	Toothpicks
Clothespins	Paper	Words and Letters
Dice	Paper Bags	
	Paper Cups	

THESE ARE, of course, *relatively* quiet games. The more successful they are, the more noise they are likely to produce. On the other hand, they involve little physical activity and, for the most part, are practical in small spaces.

BALLOONS

*Basketball. A round balloon serves as a basketball; a wire hanger serves as a hoop. To form the hoop, shape the body of the hanger into a circle, then bend the circle so that it projects at a right angle from the handle of the hanger. If a younger child is involved, hang the hoop on

NOTE: For explanation of (*) symbol, see page 13.

a doorknob. With an older child, align it from the top of the door. Each basket counts two points.

Release. Several balloons are needed. The object is to fill them with air, then let go and see how far they travel. With two or more children, arrange a competition.

Strike. A player attempts to keep an inflated balloon aloft as long as possible by striking it from underneath with his hand. Two or more players might compete to see which one can keep his balloon aloft the longest.

BALLS

Blow Ball. A Ping-Pong ball and two players are needed. The ball is placed at the center of a table; a player stands at either end. Huffing and puffing as hard as they can, the players try to blow the ball off their opponent's end of the table.

Bouncing. The object is to bounce a ball into a wastepaper basket, a saucepan, or an open umbrella, first from three feet, then from five feet, then from ten.

Bowling. A large rubber ball serves as the bowling ball, empty milk cartons as the tenpins, and a hallway as the bowling alley. If space is a problem use a small ball or a marble, clothespins or candles perched on end, and a table top.

Catch. (1) A small ball is thrown into the air, then caught in a funnel, a saucepan, a shoebox, or some other unbreakable container. If a wall is available, the ball is bounced against it, then caught in the container. (2) Two players stand three feet apart. Each has an empty oatmeal container or shoebox which he uses to throw the ball to his opponent and catch it on its return. Each time a player fails to catch the ball, he loses a point. A total of twenty-one points wins the game.

Golf. Use a small rubber ball as a golf ball, a toy club or a stout stick as a golf club, and a small empty can or box turned on its side as the first hole. The object is to sink the ball in the "hole" from various positions around it. Obstacles such as blocks and small boxes add to the challenge. If space is available, set up a more complete course, using several numbered holes which a player tries in order.

BEANS

Use dried lima beans, kidney beans, or the smaller, prettier black-eyed peas.

Hul Gul. Two piles of about fifty beans each are needed. The first player takes a handful from his pile, shows it to the second player, and calls "Hul gul, hul gul." The second player replies, "Handful." The first player responds, "How many?" The second player then guesses how many beans are in the handful. If the guess is correct, he receives all the beans his opponent holds. If the guess is low, he receives the difference between his estimate and the actual number. If the guess is high, he forfeits the difference. A predetermined number of rounds is played. The winner is the player who completes the game with the most beans.

Odd-Even. Two players start the game with twenty beans each. The first conceals some in one of his hands. The other tries to guess whether the number of beans concealed is odd or even. If he guesses correctly, he wins the beans. If he is wrong, he gives his opponent that number. The players then reverse their roles. The winner is the one with the largest number of beans after a predetermined number of rounds.

*Ping. Each player is equipped with a drinking straw and ten small beans. The object is to blow more beans than the other player does into a target such as a metal washpan or a pot. Blowers who deliberately blow beans at people or at other objects are banished.

BOOKS

*Balance. A player tries to walk from here to there with a book balanced on his head. If the book slips off, he starts over.

BOXES

*Button Box. See Buttons and Counters.
*Catch. See Balls.
*Quoits. See Clothespins.
*Roll-Away. See Marbles.

BUTTONS AND COUNTERS

Accuracy. Two players are needed. Each is given a set of five buttons of a distinctive color. The first holds one of his buttons at arm's length and drops it on the floor. The second tries to aim his button so that it lands on his opponent's. If he is successful, he picks up both buttons. If he isn't, both remain in place, and his opponent takes his turn. The first player to lose all his buttons loses the game.

Baseball. One button represents the baseball and three others are the base runners. The playing field is a piece of cardboard at least eight inches square which is divided into sixteen smaller squares and labeled as in the illustration. The "field" is then placed on a table or the floor. A coin is flipped to determine which team bats first. The player whose team is at bat begins the game by tossing the "ball" from four feet away onto the field. If the button lands in a square that indicates a hit, the player moves his batter to the appropriate base. Should a second hit follow, the base runner and the man at bat both advance the number of bases involved. If the batter grounds out, the base runner advances one base. If he flies, pops, or fouls out, the base runner does not advance. If the button lands on a line separating two squares or misses the field completely, the result is a foul strike. If a player fouls a ball three times in one of his turns at bat, he is called out. Of course, when three outs are recorded, the other team takes its turn.

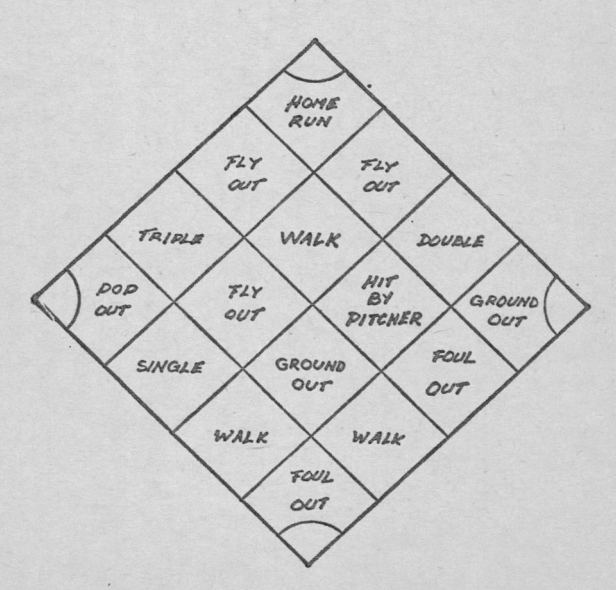

20 / THE RAINY DAY BOOK

Basketball. A button is the ball and a piece of cardboard is the playing area. The cardboard is marked as in the illustration and placed on a table or the floor. The two players toss a coin to determine who is to have possession of the ball first. During the game each player stands about a foot behind the goal he is defending and throws the "ball" into play from there. The action is determined by the section of the court in which the ball lands. If it lands partially in two sections, the opposing player decides which one counts. The action in each section is as follows:

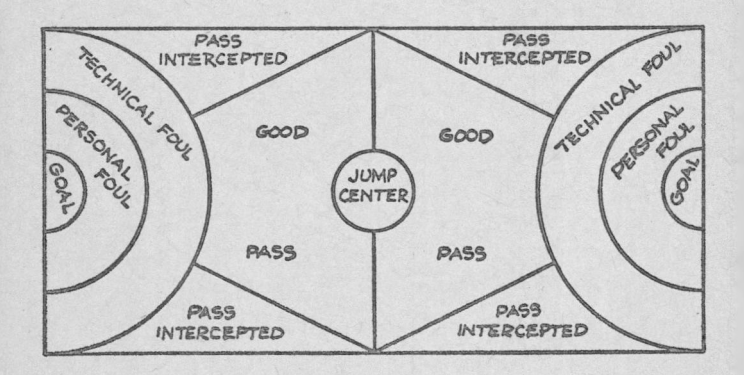

Good Pass. Take another turn.

Pass Intercepted. Other player takes the ball.

Out of Bounds. Other player takes the ball.

Technical Foul. Other player receives one free throw at the goal with a chance to score one point. If the ball lands in the penalty area instead of in the goal, the penalty does not count. Whether or not the player scores, he puts the ball back into play.

Personal Foul. Other player receives two free throws with the chance to score one point with each. Otherwise, the rules for a Technical Foul apply.

Goal. Two points are scored; the scoring player puts the ball back into play.

The player with the highest score at the end of two ten-minute halves is the winner.

Button Box. Preschoolers may like this game. Cut slots of various lengths and widths in the top of a shoebox or a cylindrical container. Then provide a pile of buttons and other objects to be dropped through the appropriate slots.

Guessing. See Beans (Hul Gul and Odd-Even). Use small buttons.

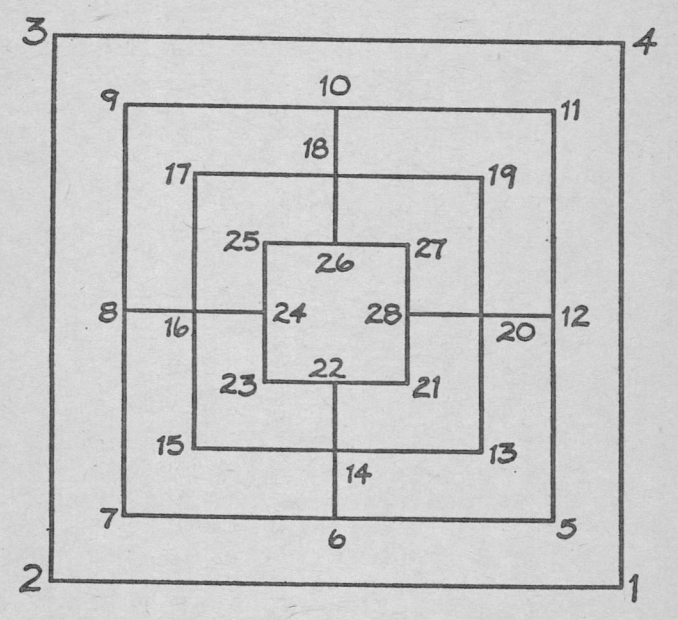

Mill. This game is suitable for two older children. Also known as Nine Men's Morris and Morelles, it was played in Shakespeare's day. In fact, he makes a reference to it in *A Midsummer Night's Dream*.[1] The playing area is

---

[1] "The nine men's morris is fill'd up with mud,
And the quaint mazes in the wanton green
For lack of tread are undistinguishable. . . ."

shown in the illustration. Each player needs nine buttons of a distinctive color or nine counters which have been cut from cardboard and colored.

To start the game, the players alternately place their buttons on the numbered positions in the playing area. The object is to form vertical or horizontal rows of three buttons each. These rows are called "mills." For example, "24," "16," and "8" would be one mill; "22," "14," and "6" would be another. A mill may consist of three of one player's buttons or a combination of his buttons and those of his opponent. When a player completes a mill he removes one of his opponent's buttons. The only exceptions are those in an existing mill. They may not be removed unless others are not available.

When all the buttons have been put out, the players continue their attempt to form mills. They do this by moving their pieces to adjoining positions. When a player has only three buttons left, he is given the freedom to move them directly to unoccupied positions anywhere on the board. But he must be extremely cautious. If he loses one more, he loses the game.

Sheep and Wolves. One player represents twenty sheep; the other represents two marauding wolves. The search for the sheep, their attempts to protect themselves from the wolves, and their efforts to find safety in a sheep pen that is far too small for all of them are enacted on a playing area like the one illustrated. To start, the players cut twenty-two small counters from a piece of cardboard. The twenty that represent the sheep are placed at the intersections marked by white circles in the top half of the playing area. The two that represent the wolves are colored a sinister black and are placed where the black circles are. The nine places available in the sheep pen are indicated by the circles with the letter "S."

Each player alternately moves one counter to an adjoining intersection. The sheep move forward on the vertical or horizontal lines. The wolves move in any direction, using the diagonal lines as well as the others. A wolf removes a sheep from the board by jumping. The sheep protect themselves by massing together and trying to force the wolves into positions from which they cannot move. If the sheep trap both wolves in this way or manage to get nine of their flock into the sheep pen, they win the game. If the wolves reduce the number of sheep to eight, they are the victors.

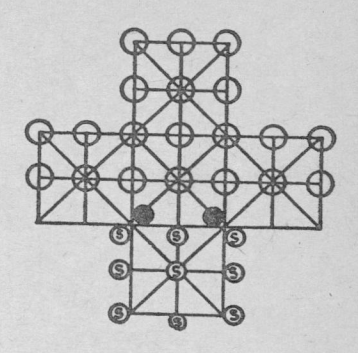

Snap. (1) As in tiddlywinks, the edge of one button is pressed against the edge of another so that the button being pressed leaps forward. The object is to move the button a specified distance. (2) A set of goal posts is constructed of two empty thread spools and three drinking straws. Two of the straws are placed upright in the spool holes. The third is taped in place as a crossbar. The idea is to snap the button through the uprights.

Sunshine and Rain. See Calendars.

Tick Tack Toe. (1) One player has five black buttons; the other has five white buttons. Playing on the traditional nine squares, each tries to arrange his buttons so that he is the first to achieve a row of three in any direction. (2) The objective is to *avoid* establishing a row of three.

Toss. There are many possibilities. In each version, buttons are tossed at a target. With one child, the game is a test of skill. With more than one, it is a competition for the highest score. Players stand three to five feet away depending on their age.

Calendar Toss: See Calendars.

Container Toss: In each round a player pitches a series of five buttons into several containers bearing different point values. Measuring cups, paper bags, water glasses, or the compartments of egg cartons and muffin tins are good targets. Also try an empty cylindrical container of the type that holds ice cream or oatmeal. The container is placed on its side with the open end at the edge of a table. Each time the player tosses a button into the container he gets one point.

Rectangle Toss: This game requires two buttons of different colors. One button causes points to be added to a score; the other causes points to be subtracted. A large rectangle is marked on a piece of cardboard; it is then divided into nine smaller rectangles as in Tick Tack Toe, and each is given a point value. Each player in turn throws his "add" button, then his "subtract" button. If the "add" button lands on six and the "subtract" button lands on four, his net score for that round is two. If the "add" button lands on four and the "subtract" button on six, the net score is minus two. If a button lands in two rectangles, the lower number applies. The winner is the first to reach a predetermined score. If his buttons land on numbers which cause him to exceed that score, he must keep trying until he obtains exactly the number of points needed.

CALENDARS

Calendar Toss. A page from a large calendar is the target. Each date represents the points a player receives if his button lands there. If the button lands on two dates, the lower number counts.

Sunshine and Rain. Tear a page with a thirty-day month from a large calendar. If a calendar isn't available create one on a large sheet of paper. Thirty black and thirty yellow counters are needed, each about the size of one square on the calendar. Have the players cut the counters from cardboard or paper and color them with crayons. The player who represents the sun uses the yellow counters; the one who represents the rain uses the black counters.

The first player rolls a pair of dice. If he is the sun and rolls an even total he places a yellow counter on the first day of the month. If he rolls an odd total he forfeits his turn. Then it is the rain's turn. If he rolls an odd total, he covers the next open day with a black counter. If he throws an even number, he forfeits his turn. The winner has the largest number of counters in place when the month ends.

CANDY

Chew Fast. Two players, a piece of thread three feet long, and a piece of candy with a hole in the center are needed. The thread is drawn through the hole and the candy is positioned at the center of the thread. The players each put one end of the thread in their mouths and start chewing. The first one to arrive at the candy wins it and the game.

CHECKERS

In case you have forgotten, the object is to capture the opposition's checkers. To start, one player has twelve red checkers and the other twelve black checkers. Each arranges his checkers on the black squares in the back three rows at the ends of the board. Individual checkers are moved forward in turn on the black squares one square at a time. They capture opposing checkers by "jumping" over them to the black square just beyond. When they enter the opposition's back row, they are crowned with an additional checker the same color and become kings. As kings, they may be moved forward or backward. Here are six variations on these rules—and six possibilities for him.

Between the Scissors. Each player tries to eliminate the opposition's checkers by trapping them one by one between two of his own. A checker is caught "between the scissors"

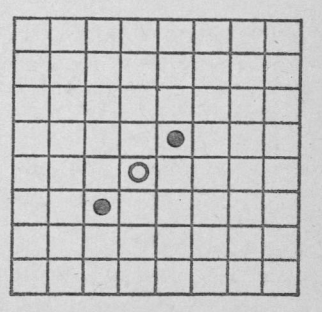

when two opposing checkers are positioned on either side of it in a vertical, horizontal, or diagonal line. All squares on the board are used. At the start of the game, each player lines up eight checkers side by side in his back row. In his turn, he may move one of his checkers as many squares as he wishes in any direction until its path is blocked by another checker. Changes in direction during a move are not permitted, nor is jumping.

Capital Cities. Each side has a capital city and eight checkers to defend it. The first player to capture his opponent's capital is the winner. All squares are used. Each capital occupies the fourth and fifth squares in a player's back row. At the outset, these squares are protected by three checkers on the right, three on the left, and two in front in the adjoining row. The defenders must remain outside their city. Checkers may be moved forward vertically or diagonally; opposing checkers are captured by jumping.

Five in a Line. Each player has twelve checkers. One objective is to arrange them so that five are in a vertical, horizontal, or diagonal line. The other is to keep the opposition from doing so. The players alternately place their checkers on the board, using any of the sixty-four squares. If no one has arranged a line of five by the time all the checkers have been positioned, the players take turns moving their individual checkers one square in any direction until someone wins. For Gomuku, an Oriental version of this game which does not require checkers, see Paper and Pencil.

Football. Each player coaches a six-man team. A coin is flipped to decide which team carries the ball first. The teams are lined up along the back ends of the board. The defensive players stand side by side in six adjoining squares in their back row. The offensive team occupies its two back rows. The ball carrier is the only king on the board. He stands alone in his back row. His five linesmen are arrayed side by side in the row ahead. All the squares on the board are used. A touchdown is scored, and six points rung up, when a ball carrier enters the opposition's back row.

Each coach in turn moves one of his players one square. The move may be forward or backward in a vertical, horizontal, or diagonal direction. A player may be jumped over by any other player, but those who are jumped remain in the game. When its ball carrier is jumped, however, a team loses possession of the ball. Its ball carrier, in turn, loses his second checker, which is transferred to the ball carrier the other team designates. Each game requires four ten-minute quarters.

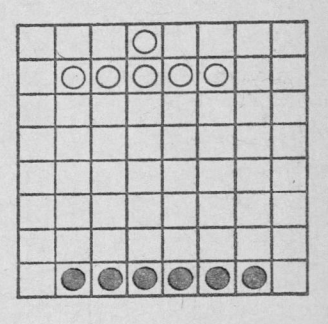

Fox and Geese. One player is the fox. He is represented by a red checker positioned on any of the black squares in his back row. The other player takes the role of four geese. They are represented by four black checkers on the black squares in his back row. The geese try to corner the fox so that he cannot move. The fox tries to evade the geese, either by slipping through their ranks or by sneaking around them. The play is on the black squares. The fox can move forward or backward one square each turn, but the geese can only move forward one square. Jumping is not permitted. The game ends when the fox has been trapped or manages to evade the geese.

Kings. This is a wild-and-woolly affair in which kings are the only checkers used and unexpected multiple jumps are the rule. Each player starts with a half-dozen kings lined up on the black squares in the back two rows at his end of the board. In most respects the game is then played as it traditionally is. In this version, however, a player may hurdle his own men on his way to engage the opposition.

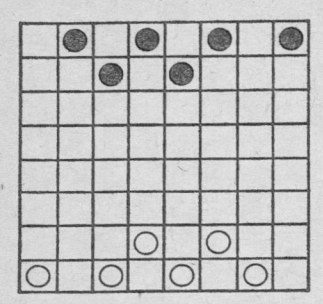

CLOTHESPINS

Bowling. See Balls.

Dropping. The object is to drop clothespins from chest height into narrow-necked containers such as jars, bottles, and vases.

Fishing. See Chapter 4: Fishing.

Quoits. Three clothespins are inserted in the top of a closed shoebox, as shown in the illustration. Each clothespin is given a point value and each player is given a set of three quoits or jar rubbers. The challenge is ringing the pins with the quoits. For paper quoits see Paper Plates.

DICE

Cootie. This is a numerical version of the game Doodlebug. Each number on a single die represents a different part of the cootie's body: "one" is the torso, "two" is an eye, "three" is a feeler, "four" is the head, "five" is a leg, and "six" is the tail. The objective is to assemble a cootie first by rolling the right numbers.

Each player is given a pencil and a sheet of paper. Then players take turns rolling the dice. A player first must roll a one so that the cootie has a torso to which the bodily parts can be attached. Before the eyes and the feelers can be attached, it also will be necessary to roll a four so that the cootie has a head on which they can go. Since a cootie has two eyes, a two will have to be rolled twice. Since it has two feelers, a three also will have to be rolled twice. And for its six legs, a five will have to be rolled six times.

Elimination. Each player writes the numbers one to twelve on a piece of paper. Then each alternately rolls a pair of dice, totals the numbers that come up, and crosses that number off his list. If he rolls a double number, such as two three's, he gets an extra turn. The first player to cross all the numbers off his list is the winner.

*Steeplechase. Each player has a button of a distinctive color to represent his horse. The race is run on a track like the one illustrated. The "X" in every fifth space indicates a hurdle. The first player rolls the dice. If he rolls two numbers lower than five, the lower of these is the num-

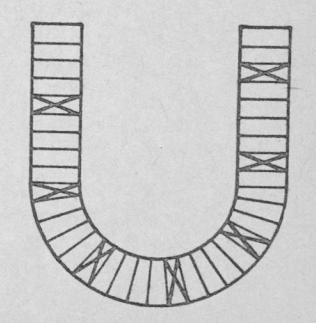

ber of spaces he moves his horse. If he rolls two numbers above five, he forfeits his turn. If he rolls a double five, then he moves back five spaces. If he rolls a double six, he returns to the starting line. If in moving forward or backward he lands on a hurdle, he loses one turn.

DRINKING STRAWS

Croquet. See Thread Spools.

Pick Up. A handful of drinking straws is dropped on a table or an uncarpeted floor. The players tries to pick up as many straws as he can without causing any other straws to move. When it is difficult to pick up a straw without disturbing another, a toothpick may be used to separate them. A player continues play until he accidentally causes a straw to move. He receives one point for each straw he manages to pick up. If two youngsters are playing, each uses his own straws. The winner is the one with the most points.

Ping. See Beans.

FRUIT

Guessing. Before consuming an orange, an apple, or a piece of watermelon, the eater guesses how many seeds are inside. He then counts them as he eats. If he wins he gets another helping.

HERBS AND SPICES

Sniff. A number of herbs and spices with distinctive odors are placed on a table. Each player tries to familiarize himself with them. Next one player closes his eyes and is presented with samples to identify. Then the other players take their turns. The one who identifies the most odors correctly wins the game.

IDENTIFICATION

In the games that follow, the player who makes the largest number of correct identifications is the winner.

Drop It. Two players jointly select a group of ten objects that can be dropped safely on the floor, using such things as a spoon, a book, a coin, a paper clip, and a rubber ball. One player closes his eyes and attempts to identify the objects as each is dropped. The other player then tries his luck.

Feel the Raisin. A raisin, a wet soap pad, cold cooked noodles, or anything else small enough to fit is placed at the bottom of a paper bag. The players attempt to guess what the object is from the way it feels.

Sniff. See Herbs and Spices.

Taste It. One player closes his eyes. The other feeds him miniscule amounts of food which he must identify. Grains of salt and sugar, a bit of cheese, a spot of mustard, a sliver of apple, and a few cracker crumbs are but some of the possibilities. Using the same items, the other player then takes his turn.

KITCHEN TIMERS

Ticking Timer. A kitchen timer is set for ten minutes and hidden somewhere in a room. The searcher's only clue is the ticking sound. When the bell goes off, his time is up.

LAUGHTER

Laugh a Little. One player has three minutes to make the other laugh as a result of his antics or what he says. Then they reverse roles.

MAGAZINES

Alphabet. The players search through old magazines for twenty-six illustrations, each of which shows an object that starts with a different letter of the alphabet. The winner is the one who completes his series first.

Telegrams. Each player needs an old magazine, some blank paper, a pair of scissors, and a pot of paste. By snipping words and phrases from his magazine and pasting them on a sheet of paper, one player prepares a telegram for the other. Using his paste pot and magazine, the recipient fires off a response. They continue in this fashion until nothing more remains to be said.

MARBLES

Bowling. See Balls.

Croquet. See Thread Spools.

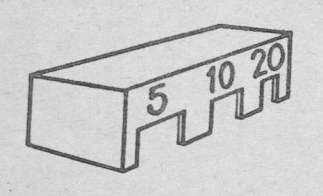

Roll-Away. This game requires the bottom portion of a shoebox. Turn the box upside down. Then cut three or four holes of varying widths at what is now the bottom of one of the sides and give each of the holes a point value, as shown in the illustration. When all is ready place the box on the floor against a wall. The object is to roll marbles through the openings, accumulating as many points as have been decided before the game. A player dispatches his marbles from a distance of three or four feet. Should two or more players be involved, each shoots three marbles in turn. The first to reach a specified score is the winner.

Target. See Paper Plates.

MEMORY

California. One player announces that he is going to California and is taking his red wagon with him. His opponent announces that *he* is going to California and is taking *his* red wagon and football with him. The first player then discloses that he is taking his red wagon, football, and space helmet with him. Each player in turn ticks off all that was announced earlier and, not to be outdone, adds an additional item. The first player to leave out an item or present his list out of order drops out of the game.

Contents. A player studies a room carefully, noting its contents and arrangement. Then he leaves. While he is gone his opponent makes a slight change in the room by adding, moving, or removing an object. The first player then returns. He has three minutes to determine how the room differs from when he saw it last.

Objects. One player arranges on a table ten objects he has selected—such things as a book, a vase, an ashtray, a letter, a baseball, and a toy. The other player studies the collection for thirty seconds. Then he turns away and tries to remember what he saw, receiving one point for each object he recalls correctly. In the next round, he selects ten objects and tests his opponent's memory.

PAPER

Chain Race. See Chapter 2: Paper.

Jerk. This is a race between two pieces of cardboard. Two four-foot lengths of string are fastened to the top of a chair, as shown in the illustration. The free end of each string is then drawn through the top of a piece of cardboard the size of a postal card. Each player holds one of the strings and positions his cardboard a few inches from his hand. At a signal both jerk their strings in short snaps to move the cards forward. The first card to journey the length of its string is the winner.

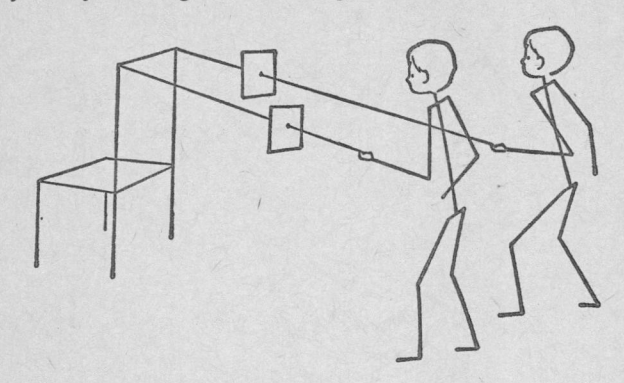

Target. Each contestant wads sheets of newspaper into a half-dozen balls, then tries to sink them in a wastepaper basket five feet away.

PAPER BAGS

Feel the Raisin. See Identification.

**Toss*. See Buttons and Counters.

PAPER CUPS

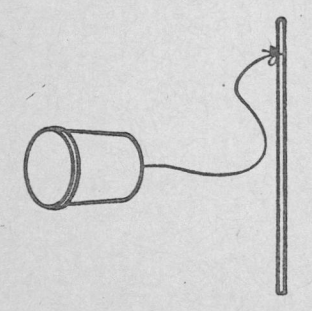

**Cup Stick Game*. The player will need a paper drinking cup shaped like a water glass, a reasonably straight stick about a foot long, and a length of string three or four inches longer than the stick. First, the cup is attached to the string by punching a hole in its bottom, threading the string through the hole, and tying a knot on the inside. The other end of the string is then tied tightly to the top of the stick. The object is to maneuver the cup so that it lands on top of the stick.

Racing Cups. The object is to blow a paper cup along the length of a string faster than the other player can blow his cup along his string. Two paper cups and two pieces of string about six feet in length are needed. A hole is punched in the bottom of each of the cups. Then each is placed on a string and the strings are suspended between two chairs. When all is ready the players line up their cups and blow.

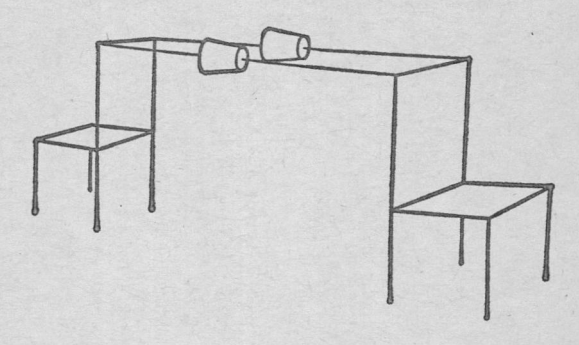

PAPER AND PENCIL

Dots and Lines. The first player places a dot anywhere on a piece of paper, then attaches a line of any length to it. His opponent adds a dot at the end of the line, then adds a line of his own. The players repeat the process until one completes a drawing that can be readily identified.

*Double Numbers. The numbers one to twenty are written so that they are scattered across a sheet of paper. Then the same numbers are written on the paper again, but care is taken to place them so that duplicate numbers are not close together. The object is to connect the duplicate numbers with lines. In linking the numbers, however, a

36 / THE RAINY DAY BOOK

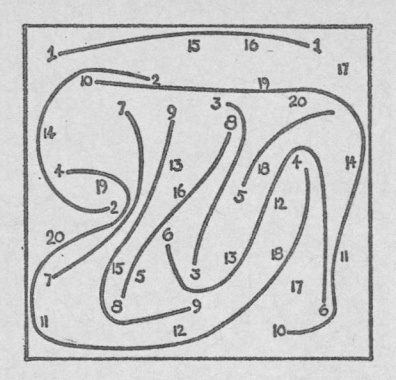

player may not cross lines that already join other sets of numbers. The players proceed in turn, starting with the number one. The first player unable to join two numbers without crossing another line is the loser.

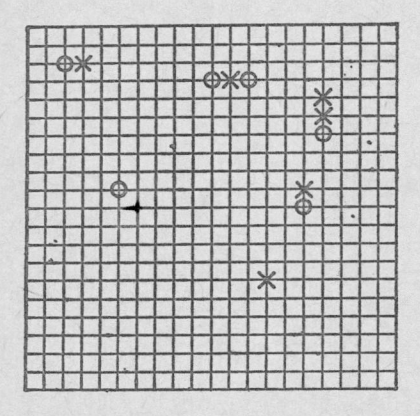

Gomuku. This is an Oriental game. The playing chart is a rectangle incorporating nineteen horizontal and nineteen vertical lines. One player is represented by X's, the other by O's. The object is to obtain a line of five X's or O's in any direction and, at the same time, to prevent your opponent from doing so. The symbols are placed where the lines meet rather than inside the boxes.

Quiet Games / 37

JS
PS
PS
PS
JS
PS
PS
PS
JS
JS

Ladder. The playing area is a ladder with ten rungs like the one in the illustration. The player who manages to occupy the top rung is the winner. Play begins at the bottom of the ladder. Depending on what seems like the best strategy, each player in turn climbs one, two or three rungs, initialing each rung as he occupies it.

Tick Tack Wheel. There are two versions of this game. For either, draw a wheel divided by spokes into sixteen segments. (1) Each segment is given a numerical value. Then each player in turn closes his eyes and touches the wheel with the point of a pencil, gaining the number of points in the segment on which his pencil lands. The first player to obtain a predetermined number of points is the winner. (2) The segments have no numerical values. Instead, a player initials the segment his pencil touches. If he touches one that already has been initialed, he receives no credit. The winner is, of course, the one with the most segments.

In his book *American Non-Singing Games,* Paul Brewster reports that the following rhyme often is used to enliven these games:

Tick-tack toe
Here I go:
Hit or miss
I'll take this!

With "this!" the pencil comes down.[2]

Triangle. Two players play this game on a triangle of dots like the one shown. The object is to form as many triangles as possible by connecting the dots with lines. The players alternately connect two dots with one line. When a player forms a triangle he places his initials inside. The winner is the one with the most triangles.

PAPER PLATES

Quoits. The centers are removed from several paper plates so that what remains are paper rings. A chair is then turned upside down and a point value is assigned to each leg. The players try to flip the rings onto the legs from five feet away.

Target. A paper plate is placed on the floor. The goal is to toss checkers or other small objects as close to the plate as possible without actually touching it. Marbles also may be used although they would be rolled rather than thrown. The player who comes the closest wins the round.

---

[2] Paul Brewster, *American Non-Singing Games,* University of Oklahoma Press, 1953.

PEPPERCORNS

Guessing. See Beans (Hul Gul and Odd-Even).

Toss. See Buttons and Counters.

PLAYING CARDS: ACTIVITIES

Tents. This sounds easier than it is. A child forms a tent by leaning two cards against one another. Then he erects a long line of tents with their bases touching. Finally, he blows against the last tent in line. In a trice, the entire encampment folds. A more advanced constructor may be able to build a pyramid. He starts with a base of tents, places several cards on top in a horizontal position, adds more tents, and so on.

Toss. The object is to scale as many cards as one can into an open container several feet away. A saucepan is a good target; so is a bowl or a hat.

PLAYING CARDS: GAMES

Around the Clock. This is a simple game of solitaire played on an imaginary clock face. The player deals the cards face down, placing them where each of the hours would be and at the center where the hands meet. When the cards have been distributed there should be four at each of the thirteen positions. The object is to move all cards of the same value to their corresponding position on the clock face. For example, all Aces should be at one o'clock, all two's at two o'clock, all Jacks at eleven o'clock, and all Queens at twelve o'clock. Since there is no place for the Kings, they are placed at the center.

To move the cards to their proper positions, the player starts at the one o'clock pile, turns over the card on top, and places it face up at the bottom of its correct pile. If the top card at one o'clock is a ten, for example, it is moved face up to the bottom of the "ten" pile. To win the game, all the cards on the perimeter must be in place before the Kings are. If the pile of Kings is completed first, the game is lost then and there.

In each of the following games, the King is high card and the Ace is low card.

Go Fish (for Three or More). The goal is to assemble as many groups, or sets, of four cards of a kind as one can —for example, four tens or four Aces. Each player is dealt seven cards. The remaining cards are placed face down in a pile at the center of the table. If any of the players is dealt a set of four of a kind, he stacks these face down in front of him. Then play begins.

The player to the left of the dealer starts. He checks his hand to see which additional cards he needs to build sets. When he decides on one, he also selects one of his opponents and asks him if he has such a card. If he does, it must be surrendered. If he doesn't, that player tells the first one to "go fish." The first player then takes the top card from the pile in the center of the table. If the card is the one he is seeking he shows it to the other players, adds it to his hand, and continues the game by selecting still another player and requesting still another card. If the card he draws from the pile is not the one he is looking for, the player to his left becomes the fisherman. The player who accumulates the most sets is the winner.

Hearts (for Two). The winner is the player who acquires the *fewest* hearts. Each player receives thirteen cards. The rest are placed face down in a pile between them. The first player puts one of his cards on the table. His opponent then plays one of his cards in the same suit. If he has no cards in that suit, he plays some other card. The winner of the round is the one with the highest card in the suit first played. He stacks the cards he has won in front of him, removes the top card from the pile in the center, and adds it to his hand. The loser of the round adds the next card in the pile to his hand. The winner then plays the first card in the next round. When cards in the pile are exhausted, play continues until cards the players hold in their hands are used.

Hearts (for More than Two). The entire deck is divided equally among the players; there is no pile. If three players are involved, one card—not a heart—is removed from the deck before play begins.

Low Card (for Two or More). The cards are divided equally. Each player places his lowest card on the table. The player with the lowest card of all takes the cards played in that round. The one who accumulates the most cards over the course of the game is the winner.

Pairs (for Two or More). This is a challenging test of how well children remember. The entire deck is dealt face down. Each player in turn exposes two cards anywhere on the table. If the cards he turns over make a pair he removes them to his personal pile. His turn continues for as long as he continues to make pairs. If the cards he turns over do not make a pair he leaves them in place and turns them face down again. Then one of his opponents tries his luck. Throughout the game each player tries to remember where certain cards are so that they can be located readily if they are needed to make a pair. The winner is the player with the largest number of cards at the end of the game.

Slap Jack (for Two to Four). A deck of cards is placed face down at the center of the table. The players take turns removing a card from the top of the deck and placing it face up in an adjoining pile. If the card exposed is a Jack, each of the players claps his hands three times, then tries to slap the Jack. The first one to do so wins the Jack and all the cards under it. The game continues until the four Jacks have been exposed. The player to win the last Jack wins not only the cards underneath but the cards which have not yet been played. The winner is the one who acquires the most cards.

*War (for Two). Each player is dealt twenty-six cards, which he stacks face down in front of him. In each round the players expose the top card in their piles. The player with the higher card takes both and adds them to the bottom of his pile. If cards of the same value are turned up, war results. In such a case, each player takes another card from his pile and places it face down on the card he has just drawn. Then he draws a third card and places it face up on the second. The player with the highest third card wins the war and all the cards involved. If the third cards drawn are of the same value, the war

goes on and the procedure above is repeated. The game continues until one player loses all his cards.

War (for Three). One card is removed from the deck. The remaining cards are divided equally among the players, who stack them face down. The players then expose their top cards. The one with the highest card wins the round and adds all three cards to the bottom of his pile.

If the three cards exposed are of the same value, war results and the procedure described in War for Two is followed. If two of the cards are of the same value and the third is of a lower value, the matching cards engage in war, and the winner takes all the cards played in that round. On the other hand, if two cards are of the same value and the third is of a *higher* value, the player with the high card wins the round without the need for war.

QUESTIONS

Eleven Up. The players start by building a tower of hands. One player puts one of his hands palm down on a table. The next player covers that hand with one of his. They continue in this way until all available hands have been used. The bottom hand in the stack is then withdrawn and added to the top of the pile. This procedure is repeated eleven times. At that point, starting from the top, the hands are removed one at a time until the hand at the bottom is reached. The person to whom that hand belongs is then asked whether he prefers the answer "Yes" or the answer "No." After he decides, each of the other players asks him three questions to which he must give the answer he has chosen. The funnier or more embarrassing the question and the response it requires, the livelier the game will be.

Twenty Questions. A player secretly decides that he is an animal or an animal product such as a lamb chop, a vegetable or a vegetable product such as potato soup, or a mineral. Through careful questioning his opponents try to figure out just what he is. The other players ask one question each in turn until twenty questions have been asked. Remind the players that their questions should focus first on the category, then deal with the particular creature or object in that category. To each question the only answer that may be given is "Yes," No," "Sometimes," or "I don't know."

Who? Where? (1) One player secretly decides that the other is Aunt Maude, Willie Mays, or anyone else they both know or know of. His opponent's task is to determine through careful questioning just what his new identity is. To start, he might ask: "Am I a real person?" "Am I a man?" "Do I have red hair?" The only answers he can expect are "Yes," "No," or "I don't know." He has ten minutes to find out who he is. (2) Using the same procedure, a player tries to learn just where he is, be it in a satellite or in the family car en route to Grandma's.

SEARCHES

Alphabet. See Magazines.

Hide and Seek. See Chapter 15: Active Games.

Hot or Cold. One player hides a coin, a spoon, or some other object in a room. The other player tries to find it. Depending on how close he is to the object, he is told he is "freezing," "cold," "cool," "warm," "very warm," "hot," or "sizzling." Using these indicators, he has five minutes to track down the treasure.

Scavenger Hunt. Each youngster is given a list of objects to obtain, all of which can be found somewhere in the house. The first one to find them all and bring them back to the starting point is the winner.

Ticking Timer. See Kitchen Timers.

THREAD

Chew Fast. See Candy.

THREAD SPOOLS

Catch. See Balls.

Croquet. The ingredients of this game are eighteen empty thread spools, nine drinking straws, and, for each player, one marble and a pencil. Two spools and one straw are needed for each wicket. The straw is bent in the shape of a horseshoe and its vertical ends are inserted

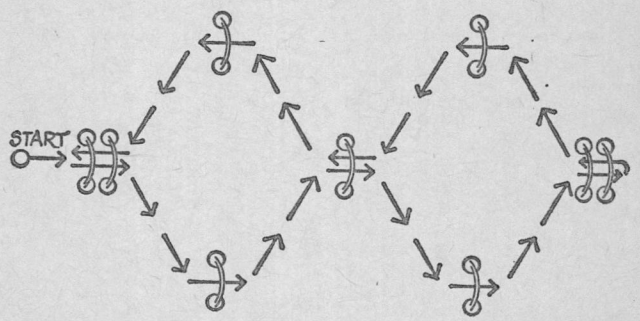

in the spools. The wickets are arranged on an uncarpeted floor in the positions shown in the illustration. If there aren't enough spools, use fewer wickets. The pencil serves as a mallet; the marble serves as the croquet ball. Each player takes one stroke in turn. The first to complete the course is the winner.

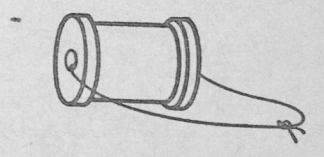

Toss. Thread a six-inch length of string through the spool hole and tie the ends of the string so that a kind of handle results. If enough spools are available, assemble a half-dozen in this way. A youngster then holds a spool by its handle and swings it toward a target such as a small box or a saucepan. See also Buttons and Counters.

TOOTHPICKS

Dropping. See Clothespins.

Pick Up. See Drinking Straws.

Piling High. The object is to pile as many toothpicks as possible atop an empty pop bottle or milk bottle. If two youngsters are involved, give each a stack of twenty-five toothpicks. They then take turns placing one toothpick at a time on top of the bottle. If a player knocks any toothpicks off in the process he adds those to his stack. The first one to successfully use all his toothpicks is the winner.

WORDS AND LETTERS

Air, Earth, Water. A player selects one of these categories. By the time he counts to five, the second player must name a creature that lives in that environment. If the first player selects air, for example, the second might reply "butterfly"; if he selects earth, his opponent might answer "worm." A particular species can be named only once. If a player answers incorrectly or is unable to answer, he is penalized one point. The player with the largest number of penalty points loses.

Alphabet. See Magazines.

Anagrams. If two players are involved in this exercise in word-making, five complete alphabets are needed. For each additional player add two additional alphabets. The players cut sheets of cardboard into one-inch squares, inscribe the letters, and place them face down on a table. Each player then selects fifty squares, which he arranges face up in front of him. With these he forms as many words as he can in a given time. The wordiest player is the winner.

First Names. The player writes out his own first name, then under each letter lists all the first names he can think of that start with the letter.

	J	O	H	N
PLACES	JAPAN	OHIO	HAWAII	NEW YORK
FOOD	JELLY	ORANGE	HAM	NUT
RIVERS				

Guggenheim. This game also is known as Categories, but Guggenheim sounds more mysterious. Each player draws a chart like the one illustrated. Next the players agree on a key word, such as a person's name, which is written at the top line on the right. Then one of the players selects the first category. Let's say he selects "places." This is written at the left. Each player then tries to list one place that starts with each letter in the key word. If the key word were John, for example, a player might list Japan, Ohio, Hawaii, and New York. After the players write their choices under the letters involved, the next player selects another category such as foods, colleges, or rivers. From five to ten categories constitute a game. A player receives one point for each correct entry and ten points for an entry no one else has.

Hangman. The first player writes the letters of the alphabet in order across the top of a piece of paper. He also draws a scaffold with a rope and a noose from which his opponent will hang if he loses. Finally, he selects a word. He puts down its first and last letters and dashes for each of the letters in between. His opponent must figure out what the missing letters are. If he guesses a letter correctly, it is crossed off the alphabet at the top of the paper and written in the correct space. If he makes an incorrect guess, that letter also is crossed off, but, in addition, a drawing of his head is added to the noose. Each time the wrong letter is chosen another part of his body is added. Next it is his torso; then it is his left arm, his right arm, his left leg, his right leg. If the player manages to identify the word before the figure is completed, he wins the game. Otherwise . . . .

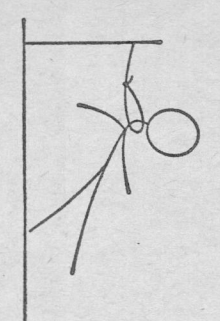

House to Mouse. The idea is to change one word into another in a specified number of moves. In each move one letter of the word is changed. Moreover, each change must produce a new word. In changing "dog" to "cat" in three moves, for example, one proceeds from "dog" to "dot" to "cot" to "cat." With "boy" to "cat" in three moves it is "boy" to "bay" to "bat" to "cat." Try "east" to "west" in three moves, "heat" to "cold" in four, and "walk" to "ride" in five. Solutions are in Chapter 17.

Initials. Each player tries to find as many objects around the house as he can that start with the same letter as his first name. The winner is the one with the longest list.

Please Don't Say It! The players try *not* to use a particular word during a specified period. Each time they forget and use the forbidden word, they are penalized one point. The winner is the player with the lowest score. To get them started, suggest "I," "me," "you," "eat," and "let."

Sentences. (1) One player reads a short sentence out of a book or a magazine. The other attempts to repeat the sentence backwards. Each in turn poses a sentence of about the same length. As they become more accomplished, they try longer sentences. (2) A player selects a word at random. Then each player composes the silliest sentence he can think of, using words that start with and follow the order of the letters in the basic word. If the word were "peach," for example, one such sentence might be: "Paul each afternoon climbs houses."

Spellbound. The first player selects a category such as animals or foods from which all the words used in the game must be taken. He then selects and spells a word in this category. His opponent, in turn, selects and spells another word. However, his selection must start with the last letter of the word just spelled. The players continue in this fashion until one of them cannot think of a suitable word.

*States and Capitals. The idea is to list all the states of the United States and then all the state capitals. Complete lists are in Chapter 17.

Stock Exchange. Each player draws a large square incorporating twenty-five smaller squares, as in the illustration. Then each in turn calls out a letter of the alphabet. All attempt to arrange these letters in their squares so that they form words which read across or down. Five-letter words are worth five points; words with four letters, four points; those with three, three points. The winner is the player with the most points.

A	B	Y	E	T
L	B	I	T	E
L	A	T	E	R
D	C	O	R	E
A	K	I	N	D

Telegrams. See Magazines.

50 / THE RAINY DAY BOOK

*_Twenty-six Letters_. The object is to write a story in which each letter of the alphabet starts one word and the words are presented in alphabetical order. If two or more players are involved, the first one finished wins.

*_Words in a Word_. The idea is to find as many words as one can in a larger word. To find more than a few it usually is necessary to rearrange the letters. In "candy," for example, there are "can," "an," and "Andy," but also "Dan," "day," and "nay." Suggest that your youngster try "ocean," "baseball," "peppermint," "crocodile," "hippopotamus, "blackberry," and any other word with lots of vowels.

*_Wrrrrrr_. The player puts down all the words he can think of that start with the letter "w" and end with the letter "r"—for example, "war," "wear," and "water." A long list is given in Chapter 17.

2 ❦ Arts and Crafts

- Bottle Caps
- Boxes
- Buttons
- Clay
- Cloth
- Clothespins
- Coins
- Collage
- Crayons, Pencils
- Drinking Straws
- Envelopes
- Junk
- Lemons and Oranges
- Lollipop Sticks
- Macaroni
- Magazines
- Mobiles, Stabiles
- Model Kits
- Paints
- Paper
- Paper Bags
- Paper Cups
- Paper Napkins
- Paper Plates
- Papier Mâché
- Pebbles
- Pipe Cleaners
- Popsicle Sticks
- Potatoes
- Rubber Sheets, Inner Tubes
- Soap
- Stamping Pads
- String, Yarn
- Thread Spools
- Tin Cans
- Toothpicks
- Wire
- Wood

THERE ARE MANY sound reasons for interesting a child in craft activities, but the most important is that he is likely to have a good time. The best place for such projects usually is the kitchen; depending on the activity, however, a basement, a playroom, a child's room, or a corner of the living room also may serve. Of course, when paint, clay, or papier mâché is involved the more mess-resistant a room the better. In these projects it also is wise to protect the work area with newspaper and the child's clothing with an old shirt. Most children need help in getting started on a crafts project, but it is only the messy activities that require much supervision. In such cases it can be enjoyable to work along with a child on a project of your own.

It is useful to have a supply box with at least some of the following items: scissors with blunt ends; glue (for paper and wood, Elmer's Glue-All; for other materials, Sobo Glue); a stapler; cellophane tape and masking tape; rubber bands; and the materials listed on the first page of this chapter. For the boxes listed, save shoeboxes, match boxes, and the cylindrical containers that oatmeal, ice cream, and salt come in. For paint, purchase poster paints; if there are children of preschool age also consider finger paints. For paper, purchase construction paper, chipboard (a one-ply cardboard), and newsprint and save shirt cardboards and brown wrapping paper.

BOTTLE CAPS

Boat. Launched in a washbasin or bathtub, caps from soft drink bottles and milk bottles toss and bob much as small boats do. To to give them a more nautical flavor insert toothpick and raise a paper sail.

Top. Impale a milk bottle cap on a sharpened lollipop stick.

BOXES

Bank. A coin-sized slot is cut in the top of a cylindrical box. Then the top is glued in place, any loose paper is removed, and the box is painted silver or gold. For a pig bank, a child cuts a slit in the bottom of a container to serve as a coin entry and the pig's mouth; he then draws the rest of the face around the mouth. If legs are desired he inserts toothpicks in the appropriate places. If a tail seems necessary he uses a pipe cleaner or another toothpick.

Basket. In one guise a cylindrical container becomes a giant party basket; in another it is an Easter basket; in still others it is a sewing basket or a yarn holder. Two holes are cut at the top for a handle of ribbon, rope, or string. Then any loose paper is removed, the basket is painted, and the handles are installed. For a yarn box the top of the container also is used, but first a hole is punched in it large enough for the yarn to feed through.

Boat. This will not be a beautiful boat but it only takes a few seconds to make and it does float. All that is needed is an empty milk carton. The carton is cut in half lengthwise, as shown in the illustration, then launched in a bathtub.

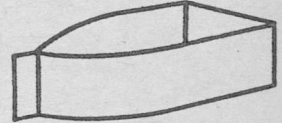

Button Box. See Chapter 1: Buttons and Counters.

Castle. A round oatmeal container is best for this project. Both the top and the bottom of the box are removed. Then jagged battlements are cut in the top of the wall. Doorways large enough for toy knights are cut in the bottom. If your child feels ambitious, he can paint the castle gray.

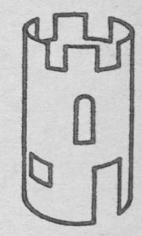

Cave, Tunnel, Bridge. With one end cut away, the bottom of a shoebox turned upside down makes an excellent cave in which to hide toy figures. With both ends cut away it serves as a tunnel through which to send cars and trains. With the tunnel turned right side up a bridge results. See Chapter 3: Big Cartons.

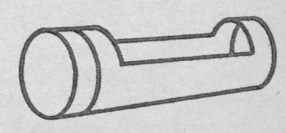

Cradle. One-third of the curved side wall of a cylindrical container is cut away, with the ends left intact as a headboard and a footboard. If one of the ends is removable it is glued in place. Your child then makes the bed, using fabric scraps as bedding, and tucks her dolly in.

Furniture for a Doll House. Small match boxes are needed. For a dresser, three boxes are glued on top of one another. For a bookcase, the drawers are removed. For other doll house furnishings, see Cloth; String; Yarn; and Thread Spools.

Peep Shows
Diorama: This peep show offers a three-dimensional illuminated scene of the type found in natural history museums. To start, one needs a shoebox, a flashlight, and an idea. A peep show created by my ten-year-old son, Peter, depicted prehistoric animals in their natural habitat. First Peter cut a hole large enough to admit a flashlight in the top of the shoebox near one end. Next he cut another opening the same size in the wall of the box at the far end to serve as a peephole. He then made a quick trip to the backyard for some soil, a few rocks, and some snips of evergreen. He covered the bottom of the box with the soil and arranged the rocks as mountains and the evergreens as trees. Finally he placed several plastic dinosaurs in position, closed the box, turned on the flashlight, and peered through his peephole.

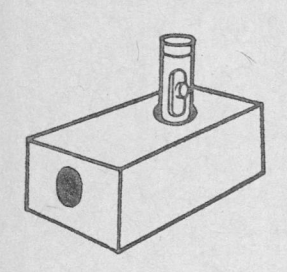

Movie: A slit is cut in the top of a shoebox an inch or two from one end. Another slit is cut in the same relative position in the bottom of the box. Then an opening to admit light is made in the top, as shown in the illustration. Finally a peephole about a half-inch across is cut in the far end of the box. For the film, a strip of

Arts and Crafts / 55

paper several feet long is needed. This can be assembled by pasting shorter pieces together. Once a screenplay has been created, photographs and drawings from magazines and newspapers are found to illustrate it. Then the illustrations are mounted on the film, explanatory titles are added, and the show is ready to begin.

Roll-Away. For this marble game made from a shoebox see Chapter 1: Marbles.

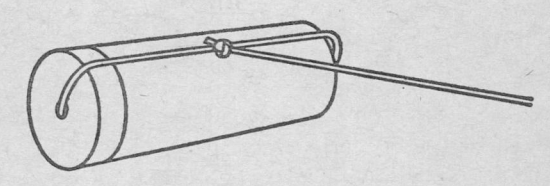

Roller Toy. This is a simple toy an older child can make for a younger one. A cylindrical container is needed. Holes are punched in the bottom of the container and in the cap. A piece of string about two feet long is threaded through both holes, a handful of rice is added to the container, and the top is glued in place. Next the ends of the string are tied together outside the container so that they form a loop. Then another string about two feet long is tied to the loop at a point halfway between the ends of the container. When the child whose toy it becomes pulls on the string the container rolls and the rice rattles.

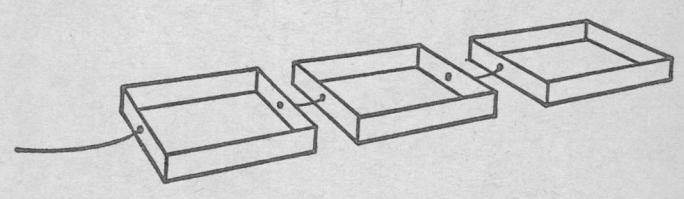

String Train. A number of empty dry cereal boxes and some string are needed. The front panel is cut from each box and small holes are made in both ends. Then the boxes are linked by threading lengths of string through

56 / THE RAINY DAY BOOK

the holes and tying fat knots at the ends. A long string with which to pull the train is fastened to the front.

BUTTONS

Belt. This is a belt of heavy cotton or felt laden with buttons. Provide a variety of buttons, sewing gear to stitch them on, and a strip of fabric ten inches longer than the child's waistline. The belt is worn with the ends tied in a bow.

Earrings, Necklaces, Crowns. Here buttons are threaded together. For a pirate-like earring a six-inch piece of heavy thread and a single button are needed. The thread is tied in a loop and hung over one ear. For a necklace, a bracelet, or a crown, the number of buttons and the length of the thread would, of course, vary.

Pictures. Buttons are arranged on a piece of cloth or cardboard as people, animals, flowers, or designs, then are stitched or glued in place.

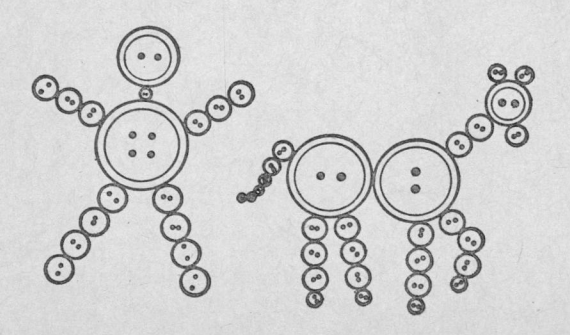

Whirligig. This button toy whirls, vibrates, dances, even hums. First a piece of string or heavy thread about a foot long is run through one of a button's holes. Then it is run back through another of the holes and fastened in a large loop. Next the button is positioned at the center of the loop, as shown in the illustration. Holding one end of the loop in each hand, the child rapidly twirls the button, using the same overhand motion as he would turning a jump rope. He then pulls in opposite directions and the button begins its performance. For a colorful cardboard whirligig see Paper.

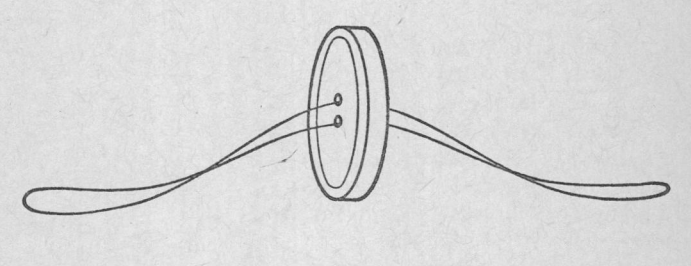

CLAY

You can buy nonhardening clay or clay that hardens. You also can make a clay substitute at home using a cup of salt, a cup of flour, and enough cold water to provide a firm, pliable, nonsticky mixture. This is known as salt clay. It slowly hardens as it dries or can be hardened more rapidly at low heat in an oven. What isn't used should be stored in a plastic bag and refrigerated.

The possibilities for clay are considerable. Children sometimes enjoy just squishing and squeezing clay or shaping it with a rolling pin or other kitchen equipment. In addition, the challenges of sculpture may attract them. Here are two other projects that may be of interest. They involve making everyday objects a child can use.

Beads. Use salt clay or a commercial variety that hardens. The beads are formed in various shapes, a hole is made in each bead with a toothpick, and the beads are placed on a tray and dried in a slow oven. They then are painted and threaded on a string long enough for a necklace or short enough for a bracelet.

Bowls. Using one method, a child pulls, pushes, and pinches a ball of clay until a bowl emerges. Using another method, he rolls a quantity of clay into lengths about a foot long and the thickness of a thick peppermint stick. He then coils these pieces into the kind of bowl desired.

CLOTH

Belt. See Buttons.

Curtains for a Dollhouse. For each window two pieces of closely woven cloth are needed. Each piece should be one inch wider and one inch longer than the window itself. A window three inches by four inches, for example, would require two panels, each four inches by five inches. There are two methods. In the first, the fabric is turned under one-fourth of an inch all the way around, pinned in place, and stitched. The other method requires pinking shears. Instead of putting in a hem, the outer edges are pinked. In the last step the curtains are gathered a half inch from the top. This is done by using a simple in-and-out stitch, pulling the thread tight, and knotting it. The curtains then are glued in place.

Pictures. See Buttons.

Samplers. Provide a piece of loosely woven cloth, a large needle, and a quantity of heavy thread or yarn.

CLOTHESPINS

Airplanes. (1) Use one clothespin as the body; use two others inserted at right angles as the wings. (2) The wings are made of cardboard and glued in place.

Dolls. See Chapter 3: Dolls.

COINS

Rubbings. A coin is covered with a piece of paper. The paper is then darkened with a pencil or a crayon, causing the image of the coin to appear.

COLLAGE

The object is to create designs with materials that look or feel interesting together. Literally anything that can be fastened to anything else can be used. Consider such materials as corrugated paper, lace paper, gift wrapping, paper napkins, paper plates, drinking straws, sandpaper, illustrations from old magazines, old greeting cards, cloth, ribbon, absorbent cotton, macaroni, aluminum foil, wire mesh, and pipe cleaners. A child starts with a large piece of cardboard, a selection of materials, a pair of scissors, glue, and a stapler. Another possibility involves cutting pictures of people and animals out of old magazines and arranging arms, legs, heads, and bodies in new combinations, the more curious the better. For a hat crowned with a collage, see Chapter 3: Hats (Paper Plate).

CRAYONS, PENCILS

Animals. Starting with two dots for eyes and a short, frizzy tail, the artist's assignment is to draw the most peculiar animal he can imagine.

Defacement. Turn a pile of old magazines over to your child and urge him to deface the advertisements and other illustrations by drawing moustaches, beards, and glasses on the people shown. Women's magazines usually are best for this purpose. He will have a lovely time. Moreover, he may get this urge out of his system and keep his hands off billboards when he is a teenager. A black crayon is best.

Dots. A youngster drops a dozen grains of rice on a piece of paper. He makes dots where they come to rest, then creates a picture in which all the dots are joined.

Dots and Lines. See Chapter 1: Paper and Pencil.

Double Drawing. Pictures are created with two crayons or pencils bound tightly together with a rubber band.

Drawing in the Dark. The artist is blindfolded, then draws whatever he is told.

Rubbings. See Coins.

Shadow Drawing. A large sheet of paper is pinned to a wall. Use brown wrapping paper, a large grocery bag cut open, or a sheet of newspaper or blank newsprint. A child stands a few feet away from the wall with his profile parallel to it. A lamp with the shade removed is positioned so that it casts a shadow of the profile on the paper. Then another child or a parent outlines the profile in dark crayon.

Tracings. The idea is to create designs with tracings of everyday objects such as spoons, pencils, combs, keys, and paper clips.

DRINKING STRAWS

Jewelry. The straws are cut in pieces of various sizes, then strung as bracelets, belts, crowns, and necklaces.

Straw Ball. To make this striking decoration, a youngster bunches together a dozen straws, then ties them tightly at the center with a ribbon or a string so that they flair into a pompon. If the ball is to be hung in a doorway or from a ceiling, a ribbon or thread is attached where the ball is tied. For balls to hang on Christmas trees, the straws are cut in thirds and the same procedure is followed.

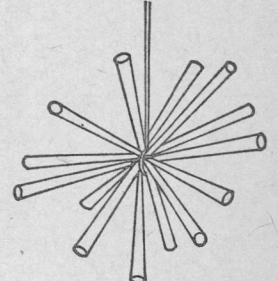

ENVELOPES

Bracelets. An envelope is sealed and one of its ends is snipped off. Then strips of paper about a half-inch wide are cut from that side. Their double thickness forms bracelets. A long envelope yields an armful.

Figures That Stand. See Paper: Cut-Outs.

JUNK

Junk includes clocks that don't tell time, light switches that don't work, and wheels that no longer carry anything anywhere. It also takes in odd lengths of wire, rope, and string, pieces of window screening, old doorknobs and furniture casters, broken toys, old inner tubes, and other things you don't want but haven't yet thrown away.

To a child of six or more such discards are the ingredients of new objects never before seen on the face of the earth. Along with some junk, provide tools, nails, a few pieces of wood, and perhaps some help in getting things apart—and who knows what the result will be.

LEMONS AND ORANGES

Spice Ball. This old-fashioned pomander ball not only looks nice, it smells good and makes closets and drawers smell good, too. In addition to a lemon or an orange, your child will need a box of whole cloves and an orange stick or a well-sharpened pencil. The object is to encase the fruit in cloves. Using the orange stick or pencil, he punches a half-dozen shallow holes in the surface of the fruit. Next he inserts a clove in each hole so that the stem is on the inside and the head is on the surface. The process is repeated until the fruit is covered. Then a piece of ribbon is tied around the length of the pomander ball and another around its waist. If the ball is to hang in a doorway, a third piece from which to suspend it is attached at the top.

LOLLIPOP STICKS

Pictures. See Popsicle Sticks.

Top. See Bottle Caps; Paper; Thread Spools.

MACARONI

Collage. See Collage.

Jewelry. Enough macaroni is installed on string or thread to create an exotic bracelet or necklace *Italiènne.*

MAGAZINES

Collage. See Collage.

Defacement. See Crayons, Pencils.

Jigsaw Puzzle. See Paper.

MOBILES, STABILES

A mobile is a three-dimensional design that moves when the air does. A stabile is a three-dimensional design that doesn't move. Both can be constructed of virtually any lightweight materials.

Mobiles. An airplane, a bird, or an abstract design fashioned from paper provides the substance of a simple, easily assembled mobile. In each case the object is attached to a thread which is then taped to a ceiling.

Airplane: See Paper.

Bird: A profile of the body is sketched on a piece of paper and cut out. Next the wings are sketched as illustrated, then cut out and pasted to the body.

Design: Seven strips, each about an inch wide, are cut from a sheet of construction paper. Five are eleven inches long, or the length of the paper; the other two are nine inches long. The strips are arranged so that the shorter ones are on the outside and the top edges of all seven

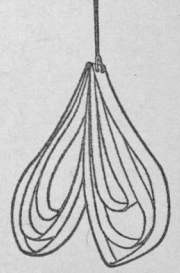

64 / THE RAINY DAY BOOK

are flush. They are then stapled or glued at the top. Next each strip is formed into a loop by returning its free end to the top, as shown in the illustration. When all the loops are formed they also are fastened in place.

Netting: One source of netting is an onion sack. Fasten the netting to a long piece of string. Then tape the other end of the string to the ceiling over the work area so that the netting hangs at eye level. Various lightweight objects are then attached to the netting with thread. Possibilities include buttons, beads, small Christmas ornaments, shapes in foil or colored paper, pipe cleaners, and paper cups. When the mobile is finished, shorten the supporting string.[1]

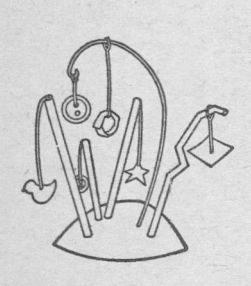

Wire, Drinking Straws: This mobile requires a base of clay. Hangers can be used as a source of wire. The wires or straws are bent at various angles, then inserted in the clay as supports. Next several lightweight objects of the type suggested above are positioned so that they yield an attractive arrangement and suspended from these supports by thread.

Stabiles. Supports such as forks, spoons, knitting needles, and popsicle and lollipop sticks are inserted in a base of clay. Then decorative materials are attached directly to the supports. Consider ribbons, yarn, tinsel, cellophane, paper cups, and designs cut from foil and paper.

[1] This mobile is adapted from a suggestion by the Museum of Modern Art, New York.

MODEL KITS

Some youngsters find a kit from which a model airplane or car can be built so compelling that they will spend hours at a time working with it. If your child is like this, have one or two kits stored away for days when the weather is bad.

PAINTS

Finger Paints. Dish out gobs of paint into jar tops or the metal dishes in which meat pies are packed. If your child wants to preserve his work use shelving paper or special finger paint paper. He wets the paper, spoons paint onto it, dips his fingers in, and paints. If the paperless method is used, the painting is done on white oilcloth or on a formica or porcelain table top, then wiped away. Or it is done in a bathtub, then washed away.

Poster Paints. For paper, use blank newsprint, brown wrapping paper, or large grocery bags that have been cut open. If you don't have an easel, use a table top. A child also will need a half-inch brush, containers to put the paint in, and a coffee can of water in which to clean his brush.

PAPER

Airplanes. In a paper airplane contest for adults sponsored by the magazine *Scientific American,* one of the 11,000 entries was created from a dollar bill while another incorporated two pie plates. However, an ordinary sheet of typing paper offers equally venturesome possibilities. A flying triangle in current favor with my two boys is an example. The paper is folded in half lengthwise. Then each half is folded three additional times, as shown in the illustration. To give the plane the weight it needs, a paper clip or a straight pin is positioned on the fuselage under the wings near the nose. In one memora-

66 / THE RAINY DAY BOOK

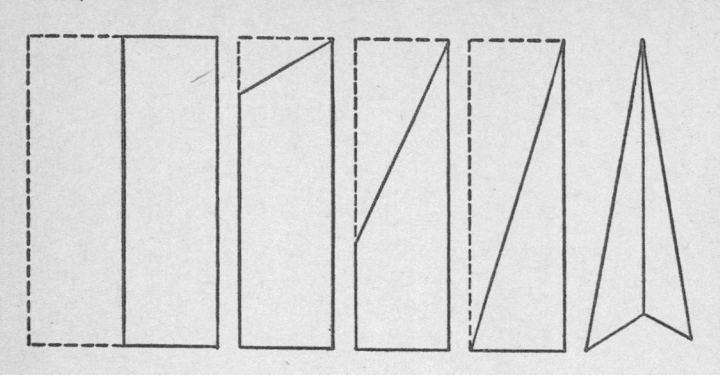

ble flight the model traveled upwards of fifty feet and remained aloft six seconds. Records established in the *Scientific American* competition were ninety-one feet, six inches for length of flight (by Robert B. Meuser, a University of California physicist), and ten and two-tenths seconds for duration of flight (by Frederick J. Hooven of Bloomfield Hills, Mich.).

Birds. See Mobiles, Stabiles.

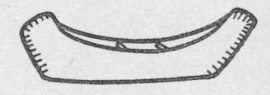

Canoes. For a canoe that floats, use one of the panels from a plastic-coated milk container. For a nonfloating canoe, use a piece of cardboard or construction paper. The paper is folded in half lengthwise. A canoe something like the one shown is sketched on one of the halves with the fold serving as its base. Then the craft is cut from the paper with the fold intact and is decorated. In the final steps the ends are stapled or stitched together and the thwarts are added. For these, use a matchstick or a toothpick broken in two pieces, which are positioned so that they spread the sides.

Chains. Construction paper of various colors is cut into strips two inches long and one-half inch wide. One of the strips is formed into a loop and glued closed. A second loop is then fastened inside the first, a third inside the second, and so on. For a chain race, provide two or more children with paper, scissors, glue, and a time limit. The one who forges the longest chain wins.

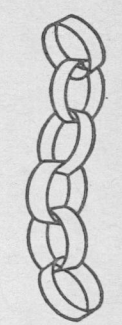

Collage. See Collage.

Cut-Outs. Using cardboard or construction paper folded in half, it is a simple matter to create people, animals, cars, and houses that stand. For a person, animal, or car, the fold is at the top. A sketch is drawn on one-half of the paper; then an outline is cut through both halves, with the fold at the top left intact as a hinge. For a house, the fold is at the side so that the house opens at right angles. Unsealed envelopes also will yield cutouts. Cut off the flap and the two side folds and proceed as described above. For a house, cut off the flap, the bottom fold, and one side fold.

Faces. A sheet of construction paper is formed into a cylinder and held in place with paper clips. A face is sketched on one side. The clips are then removed, holes are cut for the eyes, nose, and mouth, and the face is colored with crayon or paint. Hair, a moustache, or a beard also might be added. See the materials suggested in Chapter 3: Dolls and Masks. As the last step, the cylinder is re-formed and fastened with staples or glue.

Greeting Cards. The size of the card depends on the size of the envelope available. The card is cut from construction paper and folded. A greeting is then composed and decorations are added. As possibilities suggest button pictures (see Buttons), a collage (see Collage), designs cut from felt, illustrations from magazines, or pipe cleaner people (see Chapter 3: Dolls).

Indian Headdress. Unless real feathers are available, use drawings of feathers cut from cardboard and decorated in bright colors. The headband should be two inches deep and one inch longer than the distance around the child's head. Use a strip of cardboard in which a slit has been cut for each feather. After a feather has been inserted, tape or staple it in place. The headdress is fastened in the back with cellophane tape or paper fasteners.

Jewelry. Necklaces, bracelets, and rings all can be cut from cardboard. So can an elegant crown which is fastened in the back.

Jigsaw Puzzle. Have your child select a magazine illustration he likes. Then cut the picture out, cover the back with paste, and apply it to a sheet of cardboard. After the paste has dried trim off any cardboard that protrudes.

Arts and Crafts / 69

Using curved and straight lines, divide the picture into large segments with a crayon. With preschool children six or seven segments are likely to be enough. With older children use a dozen or more. Then cut the picture into the pieces indicated and turn them over to your child for reassembly.

Map. Equipped with graph paper and a ruler, a youngster of eight or more will be able to make a scale map of his room indicating doors, closets, windows, and furniture. A scale of one foot to the square will be practical. If he decides to map the whole house, a scale of three feet to the square is likely to work out. An unscaled map of your street or neighborhood is another project to suggest.

Parachute. To make this parachute your child will need four strings each a foot long, a paper napkin, a cork or checker, and a thumbtack. A string is tied to each corner of the napkin, the loose ends are tied together in a knot, and the knot is tacked to the cork or checker. To assure proper balance a very small hole is snipped in the top of the parachute. Then the chute is folded and dropped from the top of a ladder or stool.

Peeper. The simplest peeper is a piece of construction paper with a pinhole or a nail hole punched in the center. Your youngster holds it up to one eye, closes the other eye, and beholds a world in the round. For a more elaborate peeper he sketches a pair of spectacles on construction paper as shown in the illustration. He then cuts them out, places a peephole at the center of each "lens," and folds back the ear supports.

70 / THE RAINY DAY BOOK

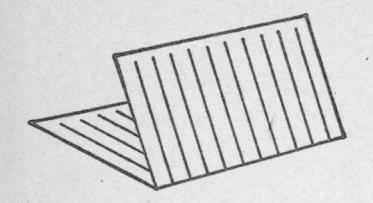

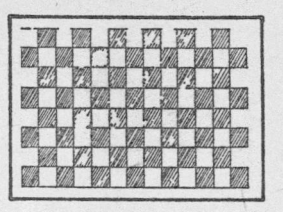

Placemat. Two sheets of construction paper of different colors are needed. One is folded in half across its width. Slits about an inch apart are cut through the fold to within an inch of the edge and the paper is unfolded. Next, strips of paper an inch wide are cut from the other sheet. These are woven through the slits, as in the illustration. The result is a good-looking placemat. But don't spill soup on it.

Shield. Using a salad bowl or a large skillet as a guide, the outline of a circular shield is traced on a piece of cardboard. The shield is then cut out and decorated, and two strips of cardboard are fastened to the back as handles.

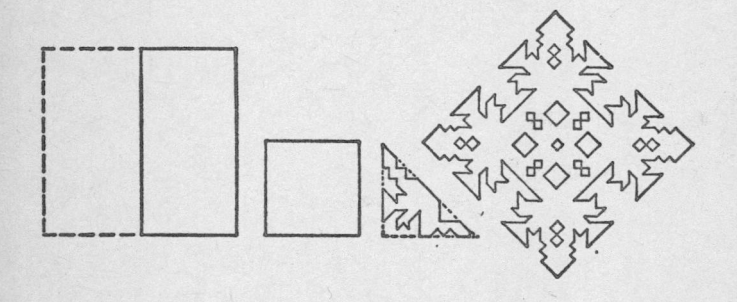

Snowflake. A square of construction paper is folded in quarters. Then it is folded again, so that one of the four corners rests on the opposite corner, forming a triangle. Finally, a simple design is cut in the paper which unfolds to reveal a snowflake of sorts.

Swish. A piece of crêpe paper is cut into strips an inch wide and two feet long. The strips are tied together at one end and weighted with a small nut. A string two feet long is tied to the other end to serve as a handle with which to whirl the strips about.

Top. With the base of a drinking glass or a small jar as a guide, a circle is drawn on a piece of cardboard and then cut out. The center point of the circle is determined, a small hole is made there with the point of a scissors, and a sharpened lollipop stick, a round toothpick, or a short pencil is pushed through.

Weathervane. The ingredients are construction paper, a large empty thread spool, a drinking straw, cellophane tape, and a long nail with a head that barely fits inside the spool. An arrow is cut from the paper and fastened with tape about an inch from the top of the straw. Another piece of tape is placed across the opening at the bottom of the spool. Then the nail and the straw are inserted in the top of the spool. To learn which way the wind is blowing all your youngster need do is open a window and hold his weathervane out.

Whirligig. The rim of a water tumbler is used in drawing a circle on a piece of cardboard. The wheel that results is cut out and two holes are punched close together at the center. Then two lines are drawn on the wheel. One divides it in half. The other divides one of the halves into two quarters. The undivided half is colored yellow. One of the quarter sections is colored blue; the other is colored red. The back of the wheel is colored in the same way. In the next step a string about eighteen inches long is threaded through one of the holes and back through the other. Then the two ends are fastened in a loop, and the whirligig is ready for use.

Holding one end of the loop in each hand, the operator twirls the string until it is tightly twisted. Then he pulls the string hard with both hands. As the wheel whirls in response, the red and blue sections turn yellow. For a whirligig made from a button, See Buttons.

PAPER BAGS

Costumes, Dolls, Hats, Masks, Puppets. See Chapter 3.

Village. Use small- and medium-sized bags with square bottoms. Turn the bags over so that the bottoms serve as roofs. For tall buildings leave the side walls as they are. For shorter ones, cut the bags down. In all cases, add windows and doors.

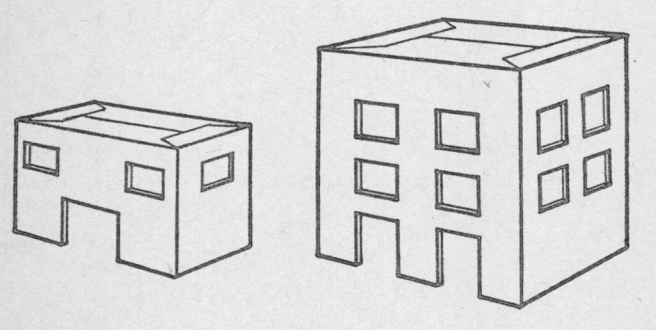

PAPER CUPS

Cup-a-Phone. This instant telephone is ideal for youngsters with secret messages to transmit. Two paper cups and a piece of string ten to fifteen feet long are needed. A small hole is punched in the bottom of each cup. One end of the line is threaded through one hole and the other end through the other hole; next fat knots are tied to keep the string from slipping through. The string is then waxed by running a candle over it several times and the cup-a-phone is ready for use. When the users speak into the cups, however, they must be sure that they are holding the line taut and that it isn't touching anything. Otherwise, the sound vibrations that travel along the string will be disrupted.

Cup Stick Game. See Chapter 1: Paper Cups.

Racing Cups. See Chapter 1: Paper cups.

PAPER NAPKINS

Parachute. See Paper.

PAPER PLATES

Masks. See Chapter 3: Masks.

Pictures. The rim of the plate is the frame, the inside a place to draw, paint, or paste pictures and designs.

PAPIER MÂCHÉ

Old newspapers and wallpaper paste do not seem like promising materials, but the papier mâché they yield is a wonderful substance for creating long-lasting sculptures of animals, people, and other subjects. It also is very useful in making masks, discussed in Chapter 3. The two basic methods of working with papier mâché are described below. In either case the object that results takes several days to dry. It then may be painted and coated with a liquid wax.

Pulp. This form is easiest for young people to handle. They work directly with the pulp, much as they would with clay, shaping whatever they have in mind. Pulp is made by tearing newspaper into very small pieces combining the pieces in a bowl with a wet paste, and stirring until they become pulpy. If commercial wallpaper paste is not available, use a homemade version consisting of two-thirds cup of flour and one-half cup of water.

Strips. This approach is suitable for older children. First the sculptor creates a generalized form in clay of what he has in mind. Then newspaper is torn in strips four to five inches long. These are dipped in water and applied to the clay. After the first coat is completed, the strips are dipped in paste rather than water. A half-dozen coats are needed. In applying the mâché, a space should be left at the bottom so that the clay can be scooped out once the sculpture is dry.

PEBBLES

Sculpture. If you have a source of supply, pebbles are intriguing to work with. They can be glued together as three-dimensional animals, people, and monuments or they can be arranged in designs on construction paper and fastened in place.

PIPE CLEANERS

Eyeglasses, Jewelry. See Wire.

Peple. See Chapter 3: Dolls.

POPSICLE STICKS

If your child saves popsicle sticks, he can use them for several projects.

Log Cabin. Use the sticks as siding on a shoe-box house.

Pictures. Form pictures or designs on a sheet of construction paper, then glue the sticks in place.

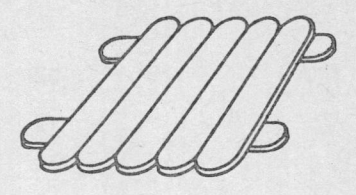

Raft. Use two sticks as supports and glue others at right angles, to form a deck.

POTATOES

People. See Chapter 3: Dolls

Printing. Here is an opportunity to create original designs, then make copies which may be displayed as artwork or used as decorations on greeting cards, party invitations, wrapping paper, or book covers. First a potato is cut in half. For a large design it is cut lengthwise; for a smaller design, it is cut across its width. The design is prepared on a piece of paper; then it is traced or copied in pencil on one of the exposed surfaces.[2] The portion that isn't needed is carefully cut away with a paring knife. The raised area that remains is coated with thick poster paint or ink, pressed firmly against a piece of paper, and removed. The print is then set aside to dry. For other printing techniques, see Rubber Sheets and Stamping Pads.

---

[2] To trace a design follow this procedure. Go over the drawing with a pencil, pressing heavily enough to create a ridge on the other side of the paper. Then turn the paper over and redraw the design using the ridge as a guide. The result is two designs back to back. Finally place the paper on the potato and go over the design once more. A light impression will be left on the printing surface.

RUBBER SHEETS, INNER TUBES

Printing. A design is cut in a piece of rubber. The rubber is then glued to a smooth wooden block and coated with thick poster paint or ink. Next a sheet of paper is laid on the printing surface and covered with another piece of wood. Taking care to exert pressure evenly, the printer presses down, then removes the wood and the paper. For other printing techniques, see Potatoes and Stamping Pads.

SOAP

Sculpture. A soft soap is best. So is a simple subject with little detail, such as a skyscraper or the outline of a car, a dog, or a cat. First, the design is developed on a piece of paper and copied or traced on the soap. For the technique of tracing, see Potatoes (Printing). Working with a paring knife, the child then gradually cuts away all the soap outside his outline. Once he has done this, whatever detail he needs is put in. An orange stick may be useful for this purpose. The sculptor's first attempts may not satisfy him. These, of course, he can wash himself with. But repeated efforts may well yield something he has every right to be proud of.

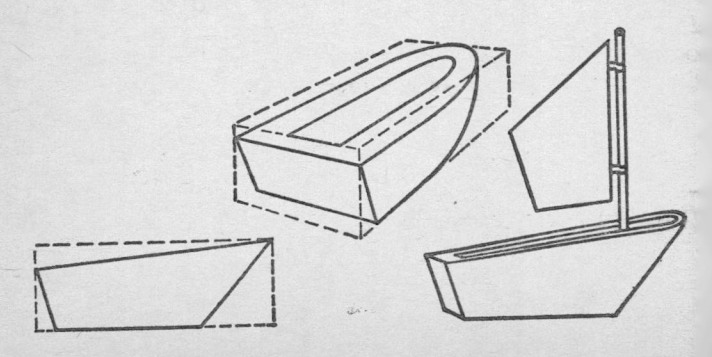

Ships. A bow and a stern are carved in the soap. Then a toothpick is installed in the bow as a boom, other toothpicks are rigged as masts, and small pieces of cloth are raised as sails.

STAMPING PADS

Printing. Using this method it is possible to reproduce the shapes of existing objects. Keys, paper clips, spool bottoms, nuts, nail heads, and anything else that isn't too big are pressed against the stamping pad, then pressed against a piece of paper. For other printing techniques, see Potatoes and Rubber Sheets.

STRING, YARN

Braided Rug for a Doll House. A tube knitter is needed for this project. If you don't have one, they usually can be obtained for a few cents at a dime store or a crafts shop. The first step is knitting a tube of string or yarn about eighteen inches long. A tube this length will yield a rug four or five inches across. When the tube is finished it is coiled flat, but not too tightly, and is sewed together as in the illustration.

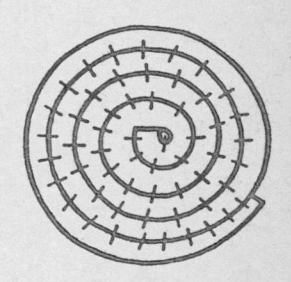

Designs and Figures. Abstractions, animals, people, and objects such as buildings and cars are shaped on construction paper, then glued in place.

THREAD SPOOLS

Dolls. See Chapter 3: Dolls.

Furniture for a Doll House.

Bench: Two spools a few inches apart are the base, and two popsicle sticks glued to the tops of the spools form the seat.

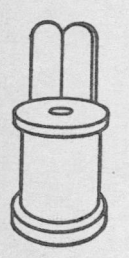

Chair: A spool is the seat. For a backrest glue two popsicle sticks or an egg holder from an egg carton to the side of the spool.

Table: A spool serves as the base of the table. The table top is a wheel-shaped piece of cardboard four inches in diameter which is glued to the spool.

Jewelry. Spools of various sizes are decorated, then threaded on string as bracelets, necklaces, and crowns.

Ornaments. Painted with happy faces or merry designs, empty thread spools become colorful decorations to hang in an entryway or on a Christmas tree. Once a spool has been decorated, a piece of yarn or string is threaded through the hole in the center. It is knotted at the bottom to keep the spool from slipping off, and the other end is used as a hanger. If plastic, glass, or wooden beads are available, add one just below the spool and another just above it while installing the yarn.

Top. Force a sharpened lollipop stick through the hole in the spool, and twirl.

Totem Pole. A half-dozen spools of varying sizes are glued atop one another. Paint, feathers, wings of cardboard, and other decorations are then added.

TIN CANS

Pencil Holder. To turn an empty frozen orange juice can or an empty soup can into a fine pencil holder, it is first covered with paste, then carefully wrapped in string or yarn and shellacked or painted.

TOOTHPICKS

Pictures. See Popsicle Sticks.

WIRE

The possibilities in working with wire include sculpting and "drawing." A soft wire such as a soldering wire is easiest to work with; however, wire from wire hangers will serve. In projects requiring short lengths, pipe cleaners may be used.

Some children enjoy working with free forms—pulling, tugging, twisting, and bending until they achieve a design that satisfies them. Those who wish to create something recognizable might work freehand—shaping animals, people, and buildings is not too difficult. They also might make a pencil sketch on a piece of paper, then tack the paper to a bread board, place nails at various points along the drawing, and shape a wire around the nails. In either case the completed object can be glued on a sheet of construction paper, positioned upright in a base of clay, or treated as a mobile and hung from a ceiling with heavy threads. (See Mobiles, Stabiles.) The addition of buttons, small Christmas ornaments, ribbons, or other decorative material sometimes enhances such a work, but not always.

80 / THE RAINY DAY BOOK

Wire pipe cleaners also are highly versatile. Here are a number of projects which result in simple playthings.

Eyeglasses. Five pipe cleaners are needed. Two are shaped into lenses, one serves as the bridge that links them, and the other two serve as supports.

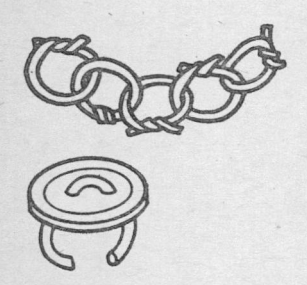

Jewelry. To create a bracelet, a necklace, or a belt, the child forms a chain of pipe cleaners as shown in the illustration. For a stylish ring, he forces a cleaner through two holes of a large button, then bends the free ends around his finger.

People. See Chapter 3: Dolls.

WOOD

Children as young as four or five can wield a lightweight hammer and drive nails into wood, particularly if the wood is soft and the nail heads are large. With good fortune and good aim, in fact, some are able to fasten two scraps of wood together. This may be satisfaction enough, but if they fasten a small piece atop a large piece, they've created a boat which can float or be pushed around on the floor. If a screw eye or a nail is fastened to the front and a string is attached to it, the boat becomes a pull toy.

If a child is somewhat older many projects can be considered. Here are a few very simple ones.

Arts and Crafts / 81

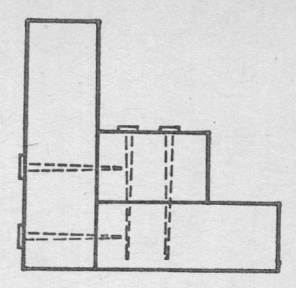

Bookends. Two pieces of wood are nailed or glued together to serve as the vertical supports. They are then fastened to another piece which serves as the base.

Bread Board. A piece of wood is cut to size with a saw, then sanded smooth.

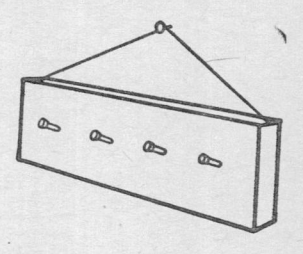

Key Rack. Nails with small heads are partially pounded into a rectangle of wood at two-inch intervals. The nails continue to protrude far enough so that keys can be hung from them. Two small nails then are fastened to the back as hangers.

Whittling. If pine or balsa scraps are available and a child has a well-sharpened jackknife, he might try his hand at whittling a simple figure. Of course, inexperienced youngsters would need supervision.

3 ❈ Dramatic Play

Big Cartons
Blankets and Sheets
Costumes
Dolls
Hats
Makeup
Masks
Puppets
Puppet Theaters
Shadows

A COSTUME, a mask, a puppet, or even a big carton gives a housebound child the opportunity to be someone else or somewhere else. There may be moments on a rainy day when from his perspective nothing could be better. A parent's contribution to dramatic play is help in assembling whatever simple equipment may be needed, but usually nothing more. A youngster will serve as his own cast and his own playwright, drawing his material for make-believe from what happens to him each day and from what he reads and sees.

A supply box is useful with this activity. Stock it with choice paper bags up to clothing bag size; remnants of colorful fabric; old clothes adults no longer want; and such things as raffia, tinsel, swatches of wallpaper, and lengths of yarn.

BIG CARTONS

A carton big enough to sit in could readily become a child-carrying plane, train, car, boat, or barge. If battlements are cut in the tops of walls and peepholes in the sides, it serves as a giant fortress. With one wall removed it is an airplane hangar or a garage. With windows and

Dramatic Play / 83

doors cut in the walls, it becomes a doll house. If the box is big enough to crawl into, it can be a cave, a hut, or some other secret place. If it is big enough to stand in and the top half of one panel is removed, it turns into a store, a teller's cage, a ticket booth, a jail cell, or a rocket ship. For the possibilities small boxes offer, see Chapter 2: Boxes.

BLANKETS AND SHEETS

To provide a spacious tent or cave, drape an old sheet or blanket over a card table or over two chairs positioned a few feet apart. Some children will spend hours at play in the privacy of such a place.

COSTUMES

Fabric Scraps. Cut pieces of fabric into large triangles, rectangles, circles, and strips. Then tie them on or pin them on, and tuck them in.

Paper Bags. Many of the projects suggested require flat-bottomed grocery bags. A few need other kinds, but they are easily obtained. When decorations seem necessary, paints, crayons, scraps of cloth, gift wrapping, construction paper, and foil will meet most needs. The costumes in this section were created by the Paper Bag Players, a New York children's theater group.

Boots: Use bags slightly wider than the length of the child's shoes. After the bags have been pulled on, install rubber bands at the ankles.

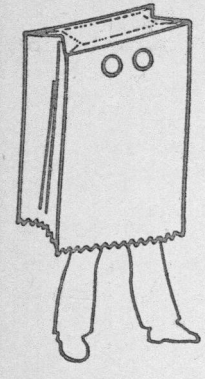

Chemise: Strictly speaking, this is a knee-length mask. It is formed by pulling a large paper bag with peepholes over one's head. If a small child is involved, a large grocery bag may be big enough. For taller children and adults, use paper clothing bags or ask at the supermarket for the shipping sacks that packages of flour, sugar, and dog food come in.

Coat: A cut-down clothing bag or a shipping sack makes an excellent coat. Cut off the closed end, slit the front wall down the center, and add armholes. If buttons are desired, use metal paper fasteners.

Collar and Tie: Use a bag that just fits over a child's head. First form a three-inch-wide cuff by carefully folding the open end of the bag under several times. Then cut off the cuff and staple or glue it at several points to keep it from unfolding. Cut the tie from what remains of the bag and fasten it to the collar.

Gloves and Gauntlets: Long narrow bags make the best gloves. For gauntlets, cut off the closed ends to let the hands out.

Muff: Chop off the closed end of a middle-sized bag. For a fur muff, fasten raffia or yarn to the outside.

Shirt: A large grocery bag serves best. Cut a big hole in the closed end for the head. Cut smaller holes in the side walls to let the arms out.

Vest: Use a shopping bag with rope handles. First cut off the closed end. Then cut open the bag from top to bottom at the center of the front wall. To wear the vest, one slips his arms through the rope handles.

DOLLS

Clothespin Dolls. A face is drawn on the head of a clothespin. Then yarn is glued in place as hair, and pipe cleaners are added as arms. If more realism is needed, a costume can be painted on or contrived of cloth. Stand the doll in a base of clay.

Paper Bag Dolls. A flat-bottomed paper bag is needed. The bottom third is filled with tightly wadded newspaper which is held in place with a string wound closely around the outside of the bag or with a rubber band. The result is a head, a neck, and a skirt. For arms, strips of brown paper are pasted or stapled to the shoulders. For legs, somewhat longer strips are secured to the bottom of the skirt. For a face, there are several alternatives. Use crayons or paints or cut the facial features from cloth, gift wrap, or construction paper and glue them in place. For a splendid head of hair, consider raffia, tinsel, drinking straws, yarn, string, strips of newspaper, or velvet. If a costume is needed, use crayons, cloth, gift wrap, or construction paper.

Paper Dolls. (1) This variety consists of several dolls which stand in a long line holding hands. Fold a long piece of paper accordion-style—first in one direction, then in the other—with each panel about two inches wide. The doll desired is drawn on the top panel. Be sure one of its hands stretches to the inside fold. Then the doll is carefully cut out. The result is a chorus line. (2) This project yields one sturdy paper doll. A piece of construction paper is folded in half lengthwise. Next a picture of half a doll is drawn as in the illustration. The doll is then cut out, unfolded, and decorated.

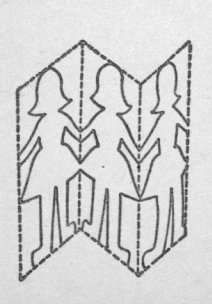

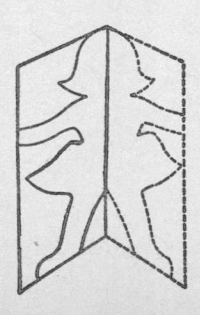

Dramatic Play / 87

Pipe Cleaner People. Three cleaners are needed for one figure. One cleaner is bent in the shape of a hairpin to serve as the body and a pair of legs. The second is twisted around the first halfway down, with its ends extended as arms. The third is twisted around the top of the body in the form of a head.

Potato People. Toothpicks are inserted for legs and arms. Facial features are added with crayon or by gluing bits of cloth, paper, or felt in place.

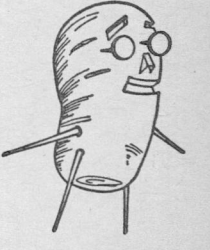

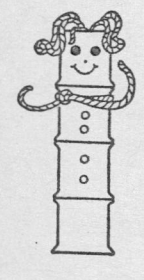

Spool Doll. Four empty thread spools the same size are glued together as a column. The bottom three are painted so that they resemble a dress. The top one serves as a face. Features are added with paint or a ballpoint pen and its hair is fastened just above. For suggestions on what to use, see Dolls (Paper Bag Dolls).

HATS

Paper Bag

Clown's Hat: Remove the closed end of a paper bag, paint the remainder black, and cut deep fringes or scallops in the top. Below this area paste triangles, squares, and circlets of brightly colored gift wrap.

Crown: Use a flat-bottomed bag. Fold the open end almost to the closed end, forming a large cuff. Then cut a zig-zag pattern in the cuff.[1]

Duchess' Hat: Form a double one-inch cuff at the open end of a tall grocery bag and squish and squeeze the rest into a lumpy pillow.

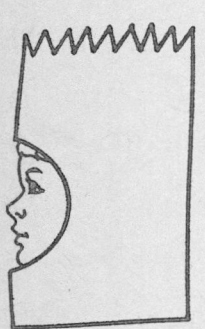

Warrior's Helmet: Use a two-sided bag. First form a double one-inch cuff at the open end. Then pull the bag over the warrior's head so that one of the vertical ends, where the two sides meet, lines up with his nose. With crayon make a mark just below the area of the mouth and another halfway up the forehead. Then remove the bag and cut a generous half-moon from between the two marks. As a last step, cut a fringe in the closed end of what is now the top of the helmet.

Paper Plate. Decorate the top of a plate with all sorts of delightful nonsense, such as ribbons, drinking straws, aluminum foil, and other materials noted under Collage in Chapter 2. Then cut small holes

---

[1] The crown, the duchess' hat, and the warrior's helmet are creations of the Paper Bag Players.

in opposite sides of the rim, attach two lengths of ribbon, and tie under the chin.

MAKEUP

Liberal application of eyebrow pencil, lipstick, and rouge is likely to meet the desires of most children. Often, in fact, the more ghastly a child looks the better he will like it. For more subtle effects, such aids as eye shadow, makeup base, dusting powder, and cornstarch may be useful. The actor first washes his face and neck. Next cold cream is applied and wiped off with a tissue. The film that remains makes it easier to remove the makeup afterwards. Then a towel is placed around his neck and another over his hair, and he is ready for his new face. Here are some additional techniques which may be useful.

For a Moustache: Use eyebrow pencil.

For a Goatee: Use eyebrow pencil.

To Reshape Eyes and Eyebrows: "Erase" existing eyebrows by covering them with thick wet soap. When the soap is dry, use eyebrow pencil to enlarge the eyes and relocate the eyebrows.

To Add a Scar and Stitch Marks: Use eyebrow pencil.

For Hollow Cheeks: Rub eye shadow under the cheekbones.

To Darken the Skin: Use a ruddy-colored makeup base.

For White Hair: Dust with cornstarch or dusting powder.

To Eliminate the Hair: Use a tight-fitting bathing cap.

After the makeup has been applied, pat it lightly with dusting powder and remove any excess with a tissue.

MASKS

Paper Bag. Pull a flat-bottomed bag over the child's head. At the first fitting indicate in crayon where the eye holes, nose holes, and mouth are to be. Then remove the mask, cut out the holes, and decorate. The mask illustrated was painted a bright red, with black glasses, a black velvet moustache, and a beard made of strips of newspaper.

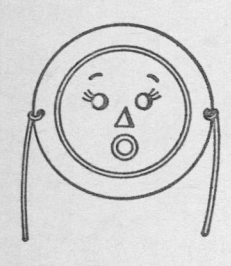

Paper Plate. What would be the bottom of a paper plate serves as the outside of the mask. Position the plate on the face to be covered, indicate in crayon where openings are to be, and cut them out. Then decorate. To hold the mask in place cut small holes in the rim and attach two lengths of string or a piece of elastic.

Papier Mâché. Several hours are required to produce this kind of mask but the result will last and last. The method is that of James T. Garner of the New Orleans Recreation Department. The ingredients are cheesecloth, masking tape, and papier mâché. To start, stretch a piece of cheesecloth over the face of the youngster to be masked, tying the loose ends together at the back of his head. To provide a foundation for the mask, cover the cheesecloth with masking tape except for sections at the eyes, mouth, and under the nose. After this base has set for a few minutes, remove it carefully. Then cover the taped area with a half-dozen layers of papier mâché, using the strip method described in Chapter 2: Papier Mâché. When the mâché is thoroughly dry, the areas where the cheesecloth was left uncovered are cut out and small holes are cut at the sides for string or elastic ties. The mask is then decorated with poster paints.

PUPPETS

Finger Puppet. The top half of a puppet is drawn on a piece of cardboard; then it is decorated. When it is cut out an additional two inches of cardboard just below are also removed. A hole large enough for a child's index finger is cut in this portion. Then the section is folded back as in the illustration, a finger is inserted, and the puppet is ready to operate.

Paper Bag Puppets

Biting Puppet: The thing children like about this puppet is that it really bites. A flat-bottomed paper bag is folded closed. In this position the bottom of the bag becomes a flap which can be raised or lowered from the inside. Next, the puppet's face is drawn on the bag. It is made in two sections, as the illustrations show. The top section occupies the bag's flap and includes the upper teeth. The bottom section occupies the area immediately below the flap and includes the lower teeth. When the flap is lowered and the two sections of the face are in place, the teeth are clenched. When the flap is raised the teeth are parted—ready to bite.

Head Puppet: This puppet is all head. Its face is drawn on one side of a square-bottomed bag. For facial features and hair see Dolls (Paper Bag Dolls). For the puppet's nose consider a raised paper triangle which is glued in place as in the illustration. If a moustache seems appropriate, install yarn, rope, feathers, or velvet.

This puppet can be manipulated by placing one's hand inside, then tying the bag closed at the wrist. It also can be operated as a stick puppet. The bag is stuffed with crumpled newspaper and tied closed. Then a stick is inserted with which to move it about.

Shadow Puppets. See Shadows.

Sock Puppet. A light colored sock is needed for this puppet. The foot of the sock is stuffed with other socks or with rags. Then a face is drawn in crayon on the sole. To manipulate the puppet your youngster places his hand as far inside as it will go.

Spoon Puppets. (1) This puppet requires a wooden spoon. A face is drawn on the rounded part of the bowl. For hair, glue paper strips or pieces of yarn in place or fit a luxurious scouring pad on top of the spoon. To shield the operator's hand, drape a cloth around the handle and fasten with a rubber band just below the bowl. (2) A metal serving spoon is used for this puppet. Facial features are added in washable crayon, which later can be easily removed. As with the puppet above, a cloth is draped around the handle.

Thumb Puppet. The face is inscribed in ball point ink on the flesh ball of the thumb. Then the entire hand, except for the face on the thumb, is covered with a flowing handkerchief.

PUPPET THEATERS

One way to make a puppet theater is to tack a sheet across a doorway. The puppeteers stand or kneel behind it, holding their puppets overhead. Another way is to kneel behind a table or a sofa. A more elaborate theater can be made from an empty carton. The flaps are taped closed to serve as a roof. Then the front end is cut away.

So are the back six inches of the floor of the stage. The back wall serves as a flat for scenery. When the theater is finished it is placed on a table, positioned so that the open portion of the floor extends beyond the table's back edge. The operators sit on the floor and manipulate their puppets through the opening above.

SHADOWS

Shadows are far more than fair-weather companions. As the cast of a shadow play they can be an intriguing source of indoor fun in any kind of weather. Using his own shadow or shadows of simple puppets he has made, a child can transform himself into virtually anything or anyone, from a soaring bird to a graceful dancer, either in wordless pantomime or in a full-fledged play of his own creation.

Human Shadows. If the shadows of humans are to be the actors, an old sheet is used as a screen on which they are projected. The sheet is arranged so that it covers an open doorway. To create the shadows an unshaded lamp is placed on the floor or on a table five to ten feet behind the screen. Except for the lamp, performing and viewing areas are darkened. The performers go through their paces in the area between the screen and the lamp, bearing in mind that the closer they get to the screen the larger their shadows become.

Shadow Puppets. It is a good idea to make the puppet theater first so that when the puppets are made they will be in the right scale. A big carton is needed. Remove the bottom and the back. Then cut a large rectangular opening at the front, leaving a frame of two or three inches. For a screen on which to project the shadows, use a handkerchief, tissue paper, or a piece of an old sheet. The material is positioned inside the frame, then pulled taut and fastened with glue, tape, or staples. The puppets should be one-half or two-thirds the height of the screen. They are drawn in profile on cardboard. When they are cut out, leave an additional four or five inches of cardboard at the bottom to serve as a handle. Since the puppets will be seen as shadows there is no need to decorate them.

When all is ready the theater is positioned on a table so that the screen extends a few inches beyond the front edge. Then a flashlight or a lamp is placed behind the theater so that the light shines on the screen through the opening at the back. Once the rest of the room has been darkened, the puppeteer is ready to begin. Seated on the floor underneath the theater, he inserts his puppets behind the screen from below, moving them about and speaking their minds.

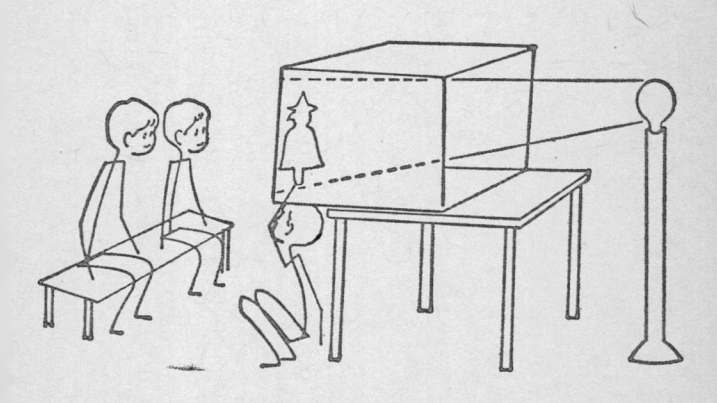

4 ❈ Water Play

Blowing Bubbles
Doing Laundry
Experiments
Fishing

Pouring, Mixing, Squeezing
Sailing
Taking a Bath

NOT ONLY do children like playing with water, it is good for them. A chance to pour water back and forth, to squeeze it from a sponge, to play with floating objects, to whip up soap suds or blow soap bubbles often will relax a child who is restless or overstimulated. On the other hand, any of these activities could create something of a mess. To keep your child's shoes and clothes from getting wet have him wear boots and a raincoat. He probably would like that anyway. To keep spillage to a minimum put down lots of newspaper. If mopping up is still necessary, he could help. He probably would like that too.

BLOWING BUBBLES

Bubble Pipes. If a bubble pipe isn't available, a drinking straw or an empty thread spool will serve almost as well. If you use a straw make a one-inch slit at one end, then fold back the paper along the slit and cut it off. A triangular opening will result. The child dips that end of the straw into bubble water, removes a very small quantity of the mixture, and blows through the other end. If a thread spool is used, he rubs one end with a wet cake of soft soap, then blows through the other end.

Bubble Water. For the very finest bubble water, combine a pint of piping hot water with two tablespoons of soap flakes or a tablespoon of shavings from a mild soap. Also add a half-teaspoon of sugar, a tablespoon of glycerine, and a spot of vegetable coloring. Stir vigorously and cool. If shavings are used, remove what remains of them.

Games. The blower may find enough pleasure in simply creating beautiful bubbles. Or he may wish to compete with himself or with another bubble-blower in producing a bubble that lasts longest, rises highest, or travels farthest over a predetermined course.

DOING LAUNDRY

In this activity doll clothes or other garments are washed by hand, then are hung up to dry or run through a dryer.

EXPERIMENTS

See Chapter 9: Air Pressure (The Dryest Cloth and Unspillable Water), and Carbon Dioxide (Soapless Suds).

FISHING

Use clothespins as fish. Float them in a basin or a bathtub of water. For a fishing pole, use a stick two or three feet long. Attach a length of string which has a long nail or bolt tied to the end. A fisherman catches a fish by maneuvering his line so that it enters the space between the two prongs of a clothespin. With the nail or bolt securely in position underneath the pin, he hauls in his catch.

POURING, MIXING, SQUEEZING

For this, your child might use containers of various sizes, a funnel, a sieve, a graduate, drinking straws, a sponge, an egg beater or whisk, soap flakes, and vegetable coloring.

Activities include pouring water through the funnel or the sieve into a container; filling the sponge, then squeezing it dry; mixing containers of water dyed with different vegetable colors to produce new colors; blowing up a storm of bubbles in a pan of water with a drinking straw; and creating a mountain of soap suds with the egg beater.

SAILING

The bathtub offers the best possibilities. Four toy boats that can be readily assembled are described in Chapter 2. See Bottle Caps, Boxes, Paper (Canoes), and Soap (Ships). Also consider inflated balloons, corks, plastic containers, soap dishes, sponges, and anything else that floats.

TAKING A BATH

To the objects above, simply add the child.

5 ❦ Attics, Basements, Closets, Drawers

THE LAST TIME rain kept all of us indoors I climbed into the attic to revisit the things we had stored there over the years. Piled in corners, spread on the floor, softened by accretions of dust, they provide a kind of record of our lives told in objects we no longer need but cannot bear to part with.

On this visit, my eleven-year-old son John was with me. It was he who spotted a scales, some bottles in a sterilizer, and a box of baby clothes, all of which at one time had been his. It was the clothes that intrigued us most. They were unbelievably small. "Was I really that little?" he asked. At that moment, it just didn't seem possible.

We also found some old Navy Uniforms. I had worn them last at the end of World War II when I was nineteen and a Pharmacist's Mate Third Class. I hadn't seen them or thought about them for years. John had never seen them. At his urging we carried a jumper and a pair of pants downstairs to my bedroom and I tried to put them on, but now they were far too small. Then he tried. The jumper fit almost perfectly. Only the pants were a little large.

Attics are, of course, only one place to explore on a rainy day. Others include the basement, the top shelves in closets, and drawers with their yield of photograph albums, old yearbooks, and family records.

What appeals to me most about such excursions into the past is the chance to recapture what once had meaning in my life. But children have a different kind of experience on these journeys. It is through the evidence and information that attics and other such places contain that a child begins to know what the people in his family were like when he was younger, and what he was like and how things were before he was born. In the process he comes to understand not only more of his past but more of himself.

6 ❦ Hobbies

Collections
Making Scrapbooks

Other Hobbies

IT IS SURPRISING how many opportunities there are at home to start a hobby. For example, there frequently is material available that could serve as the beginning of a child's collection. Buttons, buckles, bottle caps, earrings, and old keys are but a few of many possibilities. I know of one child, in fact, who began quite a good collection of insects on a rainy day by trapping specimens of the spiders, moths, and other creatures that frequented his home. If a youngster is about seven or eight, it is particularly appropriate to suggest a collection. At this time in his life collecting usually is one of his great enthusiasms.

A little later scrapbook hobbies in which a child assembles information on a particular subject, craft hobbies, science and sports hobbies, and others from cooking to kite construction begin to have appeal. Here is a listing of fifty-two that might be started at home on a rainy day. Since a hobby might encompass any subject or activity, these suggestions are, of course, just a place to begin.

COLLECTIONS

Autographs of everyday people
Biographies of everyday people
Bottle caps
Small bottles
Small boxes
Buckles
Cigar bands
Coins (For advice, write: American Numismatic Society, Broadway and 156th Street, New York, N.Y.)
Earrings
Fabric swatches
Greeting cards
Jokes (See Chapter 11)
Keys
Leaves (See Chapter 8)
Match book covers
Poems
Postage stamps (For advice, write: American Philatelic Society, Box 800 State College, Pa.)
Puzzles (See Chapter 10)
Riddles (See Chapter 11)
Road maps

MAKING SCRAPBOOKS

The object with scrapbooks is to assemble information and illustrations on intriguing subjects. There are several steps that can be taken without venturing from the house. It is sound to review first whatever background information is contained in encyclopedias and other reference books at home. A second step is exploring old magazines and newspapers for articles and illustrations to clip out. When this material is exhausted a child could write to organizations concerned with his subject for whatever material they might be able to send. These might be government agencies, museums, companies, or associations. A number are cited below. Finally, the child can read books and start keeping track of new developments.

Whatever material is assembled should be carefully organized first, then mounted on separate sheets of paper and stored in a scrapbook. If you don't have a scrapbook it is easy to make one. Use construction paper or typing paper for the pages, cardboard to enclose them, and paper fasteners to hold everything together.

Almost all the subjects suggested below are too broad to be covered in their entirety in a scrapbook. Instead it is best to concentrate on one aspect, then move on to another. Several such possibilities are suggested for each subject.

Airplanes. History. Types. Pilot training. Airports. Write: National Air Museum, Washington, D. C.; U. S. Department of the Air Force, The Pentagon, Washington, D. C.; Air Transport Association of America, 1000 Connecticut Avenue, N.W., Washington, D. C.; individual airlines and aircraft manufacturers.

Animals. Individual species such as dogs or bears. A broader category such as the cat family or animals threatened with extinction. Write: American Society for the Prevention of Cruelty to Animals, 441 East 92nd Street, New York, N. Y.; National Wildlife Federation, 1412 16th Street, N. W., Washington, D. C.; National Audubon Society Junior Program, 1130 Fifth Avenue, New York, N. Y.; the nearest zoo; the nearest natural history museum.

Astronomy. History. Characteristics of stars and constellations. Telescopes and other equipment. Write: American Astronomers Association, 223 West 79th Street, New York, N. Y.; nearest planetarium or natural history museum.

Babies. Pictures of babies. Baby clothing. A baby's first year of life.

Biography. An illustrated biography of the child, his family, or his pet. The story of a famous man.

Cars and Trucks. History. Types in the United States. Types abroad. Automotive safety. Write: Museum of History and Technology, Washington, D. C.; Automobile Manufacturers Association, 320 New Center Building, Detroit, Mich.; Society of Automotive Engineers,

485 Lexington Avenue, New York, N. Y.; American Automobile Association, 1712 G Street, N. W., Washington, D. C.; American Trucking Association, 1616 P Street, N. W., Washington, D. C.; individual manufacturers.

Clothing. Native costumes around the world. Clothing in different historical periods. Clothing for different purposes. Current fashions. Write: for native costumes, foreign embassies in Washington, D. C.; for historical information, nearest history museum; for uses and fashion information, American Apparel Manufacturers Association, 2000 K Street, N. W., Washington, D.C.

Geography. A detailed description of one street, one town, one city, one state. Write: Mayor and Chamber of Commerce in a small town; Department of Commerce and Chamber of Commerce in cities and states; history and natural history museums in the areas involved.

Government. The job of an elected official such as a mayor, a governor, or a member of the town council, state legislature, or United States Congress. Write: an office holder of the type involved.

History. An important event in local history. An invention. A battle. Write: Museum of History and Technology, Washington, D. C.; nearest history museum.

Holidays. History and observance of a particular holiday.

Indians. History of a particular tribe. Indian heroes. Indian crafts. Indians today. Write: Bureau of Indian Affairs, Interior Building, Washington, D. C.; Museum of the American Indian, Broadway at 155th Street, New York, N. Y.; nearest natural history museum.

Interior Decoration. Examples by room, period, country. Write: American Institute of Interior Designers, 673 Fifth Avenue, New York, N. Y.

106 / THE RAINY DAY BOOK

Occupations. Father's occupation. Other occupations. Check with someone employed in the field for suggestions on where to write.

Ships. History. Types. Crew. Construction. Write: Museum of History and Technology, Washington, D. C.; San Francisco Maritime Museum; Mariner's Museum, Newport News, Va.; Mystic Seaport, Mystic, Conn.; American Maritime Association, 1725 K Street, N. W., Washington, D. C.; Maritime Association of the Port of New York, 80 Broad Street, New York, N. Y.; Shipbuilders Council of America, 1730 K Street, Washington, D. C.

Space Exploration. History and achievements. Equipment. Crew. Write: National Aeronautics and Space Administration, 400 Maryland Avenue, S. W., Washington, seum of History and Technology, Washington, D. C.; San ican Institute of Aeronautics and Astronautics, 1290 Avenue of the Americas, New York, N. Y.; Aerospace Industries Association of America, 1275 DeSales Street, N. W., Washington, D. C.

Sports. History of a sport. Techniques. One team. One player. Write: National Baseball League, 2601 Carew Tower, Cincinnati, Ohio; American Baseball League, 520 Boylston Street, Boston, Mass.; National Football League, 1 Rockefeller Plaza, New York, N. Y.; American Football League, 555 Madison Avenue, New York, N. Y.; National Basketball Association, 350 Fifth Avenue, New York, N. Y.; National Hockey League, 922 Sun Life Building, Montreal, Quebec, Canada; individual teams.

Trains. History. Types. Crew. Write: American Association of Railroads, 640 Transportation Building, 815 17th Street, N. W., Washington, D. C.

Trees. One type of tree. All types in a given area. Conservation. Forest fires. Lumbering. Write: U. S. Forest Service, South Building, 14th Street and Independence

Avenue, S. W., Washington, D.C.; American Forestry Association, 919 17th Street, N. W., Washington, D. C.; Sierra Club, 1050 Mills Tower, San Francisco, Calif.; National Audubon Society Junior Program, 1130 Fifth Avenue, New York, N. Y.

Weather. History of meteorology. Modern methods of forecasting. Maintaining a personal record of local weather statistics. Write: U. S. Weather Bureau, 8060 13th Street, Silver Spring, Md.; American Meteorological Society, 45 Beacon Street, Boston, Mass.

OTHER HOBBIES

Cooking, Baking. See Chapter 14.

Crafts. See Chapter 2; Chapter 3: Costumes, Dolls, Hats, Masks, Puppets.

Kites. Construct them on a rainy day; fly them when the weather is good. See the author's *How to Fly a Kite, Catch a Fish, Grow a Flower,* The Macmillan Company, 1965.

Knitting

Magic. Write: The Society of American Magicians, 93 Central Street, Forestville, Conn.

Nature. See Chapter 8. Write: National Audubon Society Junior Program, 1130 Fifth Avenue, New York, N.Y.

Pen Pals. See Chapter 7: Writing Letters.

7 ❧ Keeping Diaries, Writing Letters

KEEPING DIARIES

I KNOW OF children as young as seven who record their experiences, reactions, and most secret thoughts in diaries. If your child decides that he would like to keep a diary all he needs is a notebook and a place to hide it. On a rainy day it will be an intriguing document for him to review and update in the privacy of his room.

WRITING LETTERS

When you feel closed in on a rainy day, writing letters is an easy means of escape to people and places elsewhere in the world. It is something your children might bear in mind. Dispatching letters to grandparents, cousins, playmates, and other persons one is interested in is an agreeable way to spend an hour. If a reply is the result, as it usually is, so much the better.

In recent months my children have broadened their correspondence by acquiring pen pals in Australia and New Zealand. This has truly been an adventure for them and it is something your child might want to pursue. Finding someone to write to in a distant place actually is not difficult. There are a number of organizations that are willing to help. Two of the leading ones are International Friendship League, 40 Mount Vernon Street, Boston, Mass., and World Pen Pals, University of Minnesota, Minneapolis, Minn.

The Friendship League provides correspondents of all ages, but youngsters under twelve are restricted to pen pals from English-speaking countries such as Australia, New Zealand, England, Ireland, and Wales. There is a membership fee of one dollar. World Pen Pals is restricted to young people of eight and over. Those under fourteen also must correspond with youngsters in English-speaking countries. This organization charges a service fee of thirty-five cents.

If your youngster wants to correspond with someone in another part of the United States, the Student Letter Exchange of Waseca, Minn., may be helpful. In requesting an application, enclose ten cents in coin and a stamped, self-addressed envelope.

8 ❀ Nature

Exploring in Nature *Preserving Leaves*
An Indoor Garden

ONE WAY of brightening a gloomy day indoors is by exploring in nature. Other ways are starting an indoor garden and preserving leaves. Here are some suggestions on how to proceed.

EXPLORING IN NATURE

Flowers. If it is the season when flowers are growing and there are some available, have your youngster put on his raincoat and fetch one or two inside. Then carefully take the flower apart to see how it is constructed. If you have a magnifying glass you will see that much more. A day lily is particularly easy to examine but almost any flower will do.

There are four basic parts. The outermost is the *calyx*, which consists of small leafy structures known as *sepals*. These encircle the petals or *corolla*, whose color serves to attract insects. The petals, in turn, contain the *stamens*, which are elongated threadlike *filaments* crowned by tiny heads called *anthers*. The anthers contain pollen. In the midst of the stamens is the *pistil*, a vaselike growth with a long neck and a small oval base. The top of the pistil is called the *stigma*. The neck is known as the *style*. The base is the *ovary*, which is where the flower's egg cells are housed.

Reproduction takes place when a grain of pollen finds its way to the opening at the top of the pistil (an insect or the wind may bring it) and travels down the long tube to the ovary, where it fertilizes a cell which then grows into a carrier for the seed. Depending on the plant, the carrier might be a fruit, a vegetable, or simply a seed container.

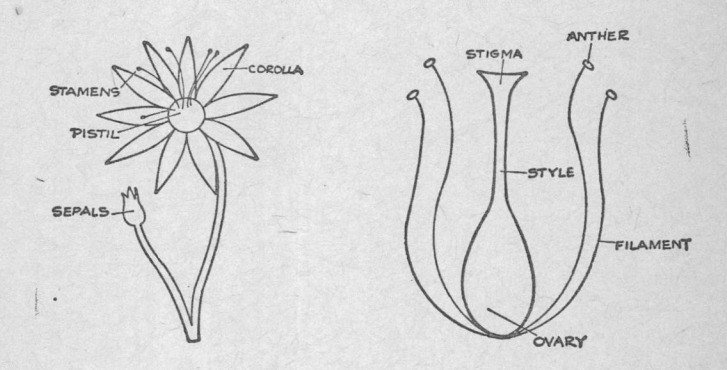

Flower Buds. If flowers are not available, perhaps some buds are. A bud contains a dormant dehydrated flower in miniature. By bringing in some branches with buds you can induce them to bloom. Doing so will require several days, but by the next rainy day you and your child may have flowers to enjoy and examine.

Select branches about two feet in length. Forsythia, elm, horse chestnut, and crab apple all are good choices. First break open the fibers in the bottom few inches of a branch by striking it lightly with a hammer. Then place the branch in a container of tepid water and move it to a sunny window. In response to the water and the warmth the buds eventually will open and their flowers and leaves emerge.

Insects. Any spiders or moths that share your home probably do not cause your heart to sing. For all their deficiencies, however, they *are* interesting to observe. If your youngster should manage to capture a spider, house it in a screw-top jar. Close the jar with a metal cap that has had air holes punched in it. So that the spider may have a place to climb and spin, install a few twigs in its cage. If ants, flies, or other small insects are available, provide them as food. A moth also may be kept in such a jar. It too will need a twig on which to perch. Feed it honey or a sugar-water solution which has been placed in a bottle cap.

Stars. A paper towel tube will serve as the basis of a planetarium which projects images of the constellations on the ceiling. Stretch a piece of paper across one of the openings in the tube and fasten it in place with a rubber band. Using a reference work as a guide and a pin as a tool, punch the arrangement of one of the constellations in the paper. Then inscribe other constellations on other pieces of paper in the same way. Be sure to label each. When all is ready darken the room, hold a lighted flashlight at the open end of the tube, and aim the planetarium at the ceiling.

AN INDOOR GARDEN

Make it clear that a number of days may elapse before results are forthcoming. So that your youngster can keep close track of developments, have his room serve as the greenhouse.

Carrot Top. Remove the top inch of a carrot and any greens. Place the carrot top in a shallow bowl with a small quantity of water. Maintain the water level and in less than a week the carrot should sprout and begin its growth.

Fruit Seeds. Orange, grapefruit, lemon, and apple seeds all can be used. Let the seeds dry for several hours. Then plant three or four of the same kind in a flowerpot at a depth of about a quarter of an inch. Keep the soil damp, but not wet. When the sun shines again, place pot in sunny window.

Seedlings. If the timing is right, your youngster can start a bed of vegetable or flower seeds and eight or nine weeks later transplant them to a window box or an outdoor garden. If he plants radishes, miniature beets, or miniature carrots, he may even enjoy an indoor harvest. If flowers are preferred, concentrate on the dwarf varieties. An empty milk carton with one of the side walls removed makes a good seed flat. Sprinkle some gravel on the bottom of the flat, then add soil, and plant the seeds according to the directions on the packet. Keep in a sunny window and water lightly with a clothes sprinkler.

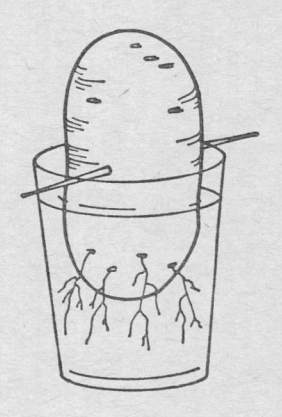

Sweet Potato. Select a sweet potato with some buds at one end. Position it in a jar or drinking glass of water so that the buds are at the top and the bottom half is immersed. If necessary, support it with toothpicks. Keep the potato in the light, but avoid a place where the sun might get to it. Be sure to add water as needed. By the next rainy day, leaves and roots may have sprouted. Within a month the plant may be far enough along so that it can be moved to a flowerpot of soil. Just be sure that the pot is large enough for the roots to spread out.

White Potato. In this case, a potato serves as a place in which another plant grows. Select a long potato and scoop it out so that it looks like a canoe, but leave about a half-inch of meat. Then fill the hollow with potting soil, spread grass seed on the top, and water regularly and gently with a clothes sprinkler. Within two or three weeks your child will have the only indoor lawn in town. He also will be the only one within miles who mows his lawn with a pair of scissors.

PRESERVING LEAVES

There are likely to be leaves to work with in all seasons—if not the leaves of deciduous trees then those of evergreens. Before dashing out into the rain in search of specimens, however, give some thought to what is available and where it can be found. Also, take some kitchen shears or clippers along. In selecting specimens obtain single leaves with their stems and small clusters of leaves with their common branch.

Over the course of a growing season you and your child might try for a rainy day sampling of the leaves that grow in your neighborhood. It also is interesting to concentrate on one or two deciduous species and follow them through a cycle, starting with the youngest, smallest, most delicate leaves, and concluding with those that finally have turned color.

There are many methods of preserving leaves. One is recreating the sometimes curious, always lovely outlines through the use of plaster casts or through crayon, ink, or spatter printing. Another is pressing and mounting. A third involves reducing deciduous leaves to the fascinating intricacy of their skeletons. In each case, label a specimen with its variety and the place and date of its acquisition.

Leaf Casts. The materials needed are non-hardening clay and plaster of Paris. The clay is flattened with a rolling pin and a specimen is arranged on top. An impression is made by moving the rolling pin over the specimen. Next, the leaf is carefully removed and its impression is surrounded with a circle of cardboard one to two inches high, as in the illustration. The cardboard is held closed with a clip or pin. A quantity of plaster is mixed to the consistency of chocolate pudding and poured into the enclosure. When the plaster has hardened, the cardboard and clay are removed. The cast is then decorated with lacquer or paint.

Many other objects in nature also can be memorialized in this way, including pine cones, sea shells, seeds, hands, and paws. However, these are pressed into the clay by hand rather than rolled in.

Leaf Prints

Crayon Prints: A crayon print is essentially a rubbing. The technique is the same as the one a child uses when he places a piece of paper atop a penny, then rubs with a pencil or crayon to transfer the design on the coin. First, the wrapping is stripped from the crayon. Next, the leaf is placed on a cushion of folded newspaper and covered with a sheet of construction paper. Then the child holds the leaf firmly in place and rubs the crayon across its length, stroking in one direction only. A detailed print soon will emerge.

Ink Prints: An ink pad of the type with rubber stamps is needed. The leaf is placed on the pad with its veins down and is covered with a piece of newspaper. The paper is then gently rubbed until one side of the leaf is fully inked. Next, the leaf is transferred to a sheet of blank paper. It is once again covered and rubbed. Then the covering and the leaf are removed.

Spatter Prints: The object is to create a silhouette of a leaf by spattering washable ink or watercolor on the paper to which it has been fastened. First, cover your child with a smock, and the working surface with a thick pile of newspapers. Then position the leaf on a piece of construction paper or drawing paper and fasten with pins. These are inserted vertically through the leaf and the construction paper into the newspaper.

There are at least three methods of spattering. All require a firmly bristled toothbrush. In each case, the brush is dipped in ink or watercolor, then is shaken to remove any excess fluid before spattering begins.

(1) The toothbrush is held with the bristles at a 45-degree angle just above the paper. Using a nailfile, a table knife, or a toothpick, the child flicks color from the brush onto the paper until the area around the leaf is covered. Be sure he moves the nailfile, knife, or toothpick *toward* him, rather than away, or he will be spattered instead of his target.

(2) A comb or a small square of window screen is used as a spattering device. The child holds it over the leaf and rubs with a color-laden toothbrush. In this case, the toothbrush is rubbed *away* from the child.

(3) For a permanent spatter printer use a small container like a shoebox or cigar box. Remove the top and bottom and replace the top with window screen. The box is then positioned over the leaf and the toothbrush is moved back and forth across the screen.

Leaf Skeletons. The object is to remove the flesh from a deciduous leaf without tearing the veins. Use this technique suggested by the National Audubon Society. First, prepare a "pounding" board by tacking a thick square of old toweling or carpeting to a piece of wood. Then position a freshly picked leaf on the board. Remove the flesh by gently tapping the leaf with a hair brush or a shoe brush. To speed things along turn the leaf over every so often. When the skeleton is free of flesh, press it as you would a leaf. Then mount it next to a leaf of the same species and size.

Mounted Leaves. With a deciduous leaf the first step is pressing and drying. This may take several days. The leaf is placed between several layers of newspaper weighted with heavy books. Then each day the newspaper is changed until the specimen is dry. When a leaf is ready to be mounted, it is carefully coated with **neutral** shoe polish or wax to preserve its color, then is pasted on a piece of construction paper or cardboard and covered with clear plastic or waxed paper.

9 ❧ Science Experiments

Air Pressure
Balance
Calcium
Carbon Dioxide
Crystals
Inertia
Magnification
Sound

WHEN A button bounces again and again, when a bone bends, when a thread dances, it all *seems* mysterious enough. Yet the button, the bone, and the thread behave the way they do in line with everyday natural laws. Here is how to perform these simple experiments and more than a dozen others.

AIR PRESSURE

The Clicking Dime. In addition to the dime, all that is needed is an empty soft drink bottle. The bottle and the air it contains are chilled in the refrigerator for five minutes. The rim of the bottle is then lightly coated with petroleum jelly and the opening is covered with a dime. Next the cool air inside is warmed by rubbing the bottle with both hands. As the air warms, it expands, driving out excess air for which there no longer is room. The escaping air lifts the dime, which falls back, rises, and falls again, quietly clicking as it does.

The Dryest Cloth. In this experiment a handkerchief is submerged in water but comes out dry. A large graduate or bowl is filled with water. Then a handkerchief is tucked into the bottom of a drinking glass, and the glass is turned upside down and pushed straight down into the water. After several seconds the glass is removed. The handkerchief, protected by a cushion of air in the glass, is as dry as ever.

The Penetrating Straw. The strength of air is used to puncture a raw potato with an ordinary drinking straw. The potato is placed on a table. The child then grasps the straw about halfway down, pinching it between his thumb and forefinger, and strikes the potato with the bottom end. The harder he does so, the deeper the straw penetrates. What gives the straw its new strength is the air that becomes trapped inside when it makes contact with the potato. Like all air at sea level it exerts about fifteen pounds of pressure per square inch.

Unspillable Water. A drinking glass or paper tumbler is filled to the brim with water. The glass is then tightly covered with a piece of paper or cardboard. With the cover held in place by the palm of one hand, the glass is quickly turned upside down. Then the hand is removed. If all is well, the air pressure exerted from below holds the cover in place and keeps the water from spilling. Of course, one performs this experiment over a sink.

BALANCE

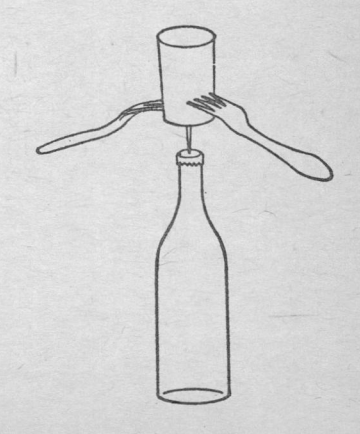

Beautiful Balance. The object is to balance a cork with two table forks inserted in it on a nail which in turn stands on the cap of a soda pop bottle. It may seem impossible, but actually it is rather easy. The two forks are inserted in the cork as the illustration shows. Next the nail is inserted at the center of the bottom of the cork. If the other end of the nail is then positioned precisely at the center of the bottle cap, the nail will support the cork and the forks without a tremor. With practice your child also may be able to balance the nailhead on the tip of his forefinger. In a similar experiment the nail and its burden are balanced on the rim of a drinking glass. This also seems more difficult than it is. In this case, the center of balance is near the nail head.

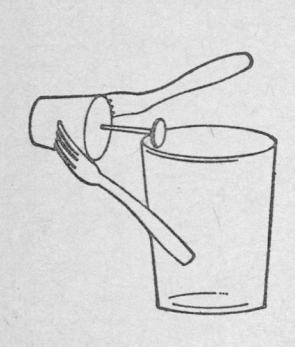

CALCIUM

The Bendable Bone. This is a good experiment to start on a rainy day, but it may take as much as another day before it can be completed. A firm, uncracked chicken bone and some vinegar are needed. The bone is soaked for twelve hours in a bowl of vinegar. During this period the acid in the vinegar dissolves the calcium that gives the bone its rigidity. The result is a rubberlike bone that twists and turns, bends and unbends with the greatest of ease.

CARBON DIOXIDE

The Bouncing Button. A drinking glass, a shirt button, and a special fluid are needed. There are two fluids to choose from. One is a carbonated soft drink. The other consists of two teaspoons of baking soda (sodium bicarbonate) and a healthy splash of vinegar in a glass of tap water. The combination releases carbon dioxide bubbles that fizz wildly. The shirt button is then dropped to the bottom of the glass. It soon will rise, then fall, then rise again, continuing its curious journey for at least ten minutes more.

With a little experience your youngster learns just how long the button stays down and how long it remains on the surface. He then will be able to issue commands such as "Rise!" and "Descend!" and the button will appear to obey. The bubbles are what keeps the button moving. When it attracts enough bubbles they carry it to the surface. When enough bubbles burst, it falls for lack of support.

POP Bottle. Baking soda, vinegar, tap water, a narrow-necked bottle, and a cork are the ingredients of this experiment. Add two tablespoons of baking soda to the bottle. Then add a mixture of four tablespoons of vinegar and four tablespoons of water. Immediately put the cork in place, but not too tightly. When the solution has generated more than enough carbon dioxide to fill the bottle, the gas will drive the cork into the air with a resounding—POP!

Soapless Suds. Place two tablespoons of baking soda in a drinking glass. Then add four tablespoons of vinegar, and stand back. In a matter of seconds froth will rise up and out of the glass.

CRYSTALS

Crystals are solid substances that occur in beautiful geometric forms. Diamonds and other jewels are crystals. So are such common household items as salt, sugar, alum, and borax. However, they consist of such small grains that it is difficult to see what they actually look like. These experiments make it possible to do so.

Crystal Candy. See Chapter 14: Candy Recipes (Rock Candy).

A Garden of Crystals. This project should yield one of the loveliest and fastest-growing gardens your child has ever seen. As a base for the garden use a half-dozen charcoal briquettes or an old brick. You also will need the following: a tablespoon of ammonia water and a quarter of a cup each of salt, liquid laundry bluing, and tap water. Place the briquettes in a baking dish, mix the other ingredients, and pour them on the briquettes. Then move the container to a warm location where it will not be disturbed. In as little as an hour white crystals may begin to form. In a day or two the garden should be ablaze with them. For a garden of colored crystals add ink or vegetable dye to the mixture. To keep the garden growing feed it a tablespoon of ammonia once a week.

One Enormous Crystal. Using this method, you and your child could produce a crystal of remarkable size. Half-fill a pint jar with water. Then stir in either borax, alum, or sugar a teaspoonful at a time. Be sure that each spoonful is completely dissolved before adding another. Continue until a spoonful will not dissolve. Then pour the contents of the jar into a saucepan and heat until the undissolved material enters the solution. When the solution has cooled add a little to a dish. Place what is left in a jar and close it tightly. When an attractive crystal forms in the dish pick it up carefully in the spoon and drop it in the jar. If the jar is left uncovered and undisturbed, the crystal soon will attract other crystals and grow and grow. Finally remove the crystal from the jar, wash it in cold water, and place it on a paper towel to dry.

INERTIA

The Puzzling Dime. A dime is placed on a table covered by a tablecloth. A nickel is placed on either side of the dime. A glass tumbler is then turned upside down and positioned so that it covers the dime and is supported slightly above the level of the table by the two nickels. The problem is moving the dime out from under the tumbler without touching either the tumbler or the nickels on which it rests. The solution requires the use of inertia. To move the dime your youngster scratches the cloth near the rim of the glass with his fingernail. Each time this is done the cloth and the dime both move forward. The cloth springs back but the inertia holds the dime in place. With enough scratching the dime finally emerges from under the glass.

Six Calm Coins. The object it to remove the bottom coin from a pile of six or more coins of the same denomination without touching or upsetting the rest of the pile. A simple kitchen knife does the trick. The coins are stacked a few inches from the edge of a table. Then the blade of the knife is slid rapidly across the surface so that it vigorously strikes the bottom coin. The impact forces the coin out from under. Inertia prevents the rest of the coins from following along and keeps the pile intact.

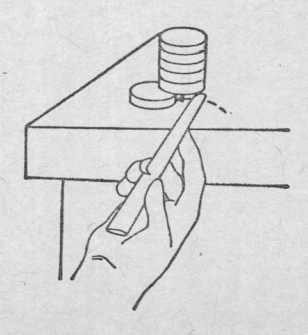

MAGNIFICATION

The Clear Eye. Through the clear eye of a magnifying glass a child can see ordinary things in a way he otherwise could not. Suggest that he examine grains of salt, sugar and pepper, a coin, a stamp, a goldfish, a hair, a gob of peanut butter, the fabric in your slipcovers, the wood in the floor, a picture in a magazine, a page in a book.

SOUND

The Silent Bell. With the help of a four-foot length of string, an ordinary spoon will yield a beautiful chime, but only one person at a time can hear it. The center of the string is fastened to the handle of the spoon so that two equal lengths of string remain. The child places the two loose ends in his ears stethoscope-style. He then bends from the waist and swings the spoon to that it strikes a chair or the edge of a table. The resulting vibrations travel along the string to his ears. When they arrive, a chime sounds.

10 ❈ Puzzles

Checker Puzzles *Paper and Pencil Puzzles*
Cut-Out Puzzles *Secret Writing*
Number Puzzles *Toothpick Puzzles*

YOUR YOUNGSTER may find it interesting to know the great age of some of the challenges you set before him. Cut-out puzzles like those in this chapter are said to be Chinese in origin and over 4,000 years old. Magic squares of the type included are known to have occupied the Egyptians and Greeks over 2,000 years ago. These puzzles are, of course, just as puzzling today. However, youngsters of eight or over should be able to handle them and all the other puzzles in this chapter as well. There are several that younger children also may be able to work out. Solutions are in Chapter 17.

CHECKER PUZZLES

If checkers aren't available use buttons, beans, coins, or homemade counters. If a checkerboard is lacking, draw one on a piece of paper.

*Lineup. Eight checkers are needed. The challenge is to arrange them on a checkerboard so that only one checker is in any vertical, horizontal, or diagonal line of squares.

*Middleman. Three checkers are placed in a row. The object is to move one of the two outside checkers to the middle position without moving the checker already there.

Remove. Three checkers are arranged side by side in one row, four in the next row, five in the next. In his turn each player removes as many checkers as he wishes from any one row. The player who maneuvers things so that he removes the last checker from the board is the winner.

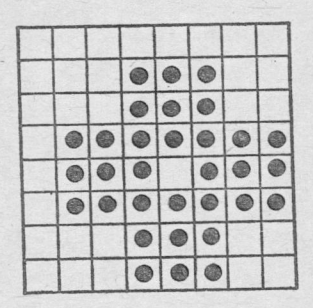

*Solitaire. Thirty-two checkers are arranged in a cross with the center square empty, as shown in the illustration. Through horizontal and vertical jumps, the player clears the board of all the checkers but one. When the last jump is made the remaining checker must be in the center square.

*Vice-Versa. The playing area is a horizontal line of seven adjoining squares. Three red checkers are placed in the three squares at the left. Three black checkers are placed in the three squares at the right. The square in the middle is left empty. The object is to reverse the positions the red and black checkers occupy. First a checker of one color is played, then a checker of the other color. It may be moved one square or jumped over another checker. Backward moves are not permitted. Between fifteen and twenty moves are needed to transfer the checkers to their new positions.

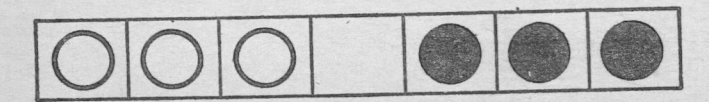

Puzzles / 127

CUT-OUT PUZZLES

When properly assembled the pieces at the left form the figure at the right. Reproduce on paper or cardboard a large version of the figure to be assembled. Then cut it apart as indicated, shuffle the pieces, and set your child to work. The first puzzle is the easiest. The last is the hardest.

Form a Square

Form the Letter T

Form the Letter F

NUMBER PUZZLES

Calculations

Any Number: One player thinks of a number, but does not reveal it. The other guesses it is five. To prove it, he asks the first player to add seven to the number, multiply his total by two, subtract four, divide by two, and then subtract the number he started with. No matter what the original number, the answer always will be five.

Number 320: One player selects a number, but does not tell what it is. The other player asks him to multiply the number by two, add four, multiply by five, add twelve, and finally multiply by ten. When the result of these calculations is announced, the other player subtracts 320, then drops the final two zeros from his results. If everybody's arithmetic is correct, what remains is the number originally selected.

Your Age: One player tries to guess the age of another, using the following method. He asks the other person to multiply his age by three, add six, and divide by three. When he has the result, he subtracts two from it, and announces the player's age.

Your Favorite Number: The first player writes the numbers one through nine in a line on a piece of paper, but leaves out the number eight. He asks the second player to select his favorite number from among those listed and multiplies that number by nine. If the number selected is six, the result, of course, is fifty-four. The first player then multiplies his line of numbers——12345679——by fifty-four. The result is a number consisting only of sixes. If a favorite number is four, the multiplier is thirty-six, and the result is all fours. In every case, the multiplier yields a line of favorite numbers.

Magic Squares. Two magic squares are shown in the illustrations. The idea is to select numbers from one to nine and arrange them in each of the empty compartments so that every line—whether vertical, horizontal, or diagonal—adds to the same total. In the first square the total required is fifteen. In the second square it is twenty-one.

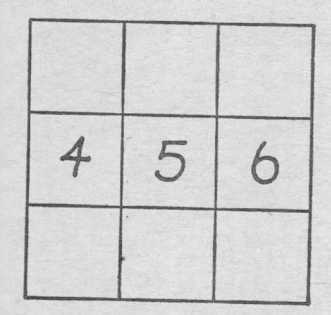

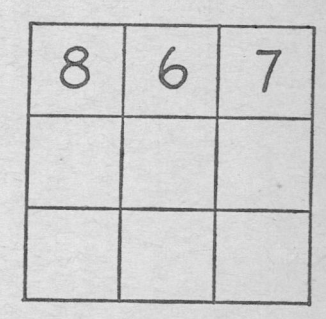

4	5	6

8	6	7

Missing Numbers. Beginners in addition, subtraction, and multiplication will be able to handle these puzzles. The task is to identify the missing digits. To devise other puzzles like these, complete a series of arithmetic problems your child can handle, then drop one or more digits in each line.

```
 Addition        Subtraction      Multiplication
  3 - 2            7 1 -             9 - 0
  6 - -           - 2 4              4 -
  7 - 2          -------            -------
 -------          5 8 6               9 2 0
 1 6 6 7                            3 - 8 0
                                   ---------
                                    3 7 7 2 0
```

PAPER AND PENCIL PUZZLES

Don't Lift the Pencil. The goal is to draw a diagram without taking the pencil from the paper or going back over a line. Here are three puzzles to try. Once these have been solved, make up some of your own.

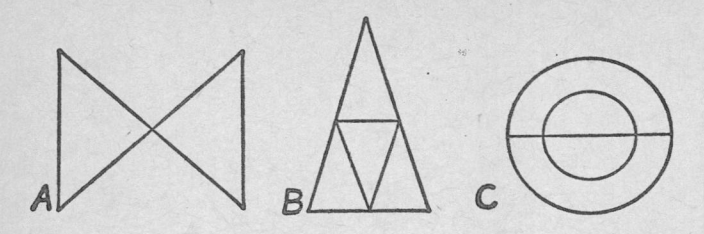

Lines

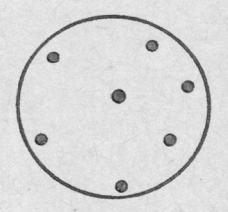

Three-Line Puzzle: The objective is to enclose each of the seven dots in the circle in its own compartment by drawing straight lines across the circle. Only three lines are needed to separate each dot from the others.

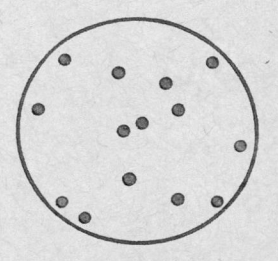

Six-Line Puzzle: This is a more complicated task. Six lines are needed to separate fourteen dots.

SECRET WRITING

Codes. Almost anybody can create a secret code. Here are three to prime the pump.

Code 1: A key letter is added at the end of each word. Then the entire message is run together as one word and redivided into three-letter words. If the key letter were "A," I LOVE YOU TRULY would read IALOVEAYOUATRULYA. Divided into three-letter words, it would be IAL OVE AYO UAT RUL YA.

Code 2: Each letter of the alphabet is represented by a numeral starting with the number 1. Every fourth letter the number is increased by one. For example, A is 1; B, 2; C, 3; D, 5; E, 6; F, 7; G,9; and so on. Write out the entire code, then have your child try it. To make the code more confusing suggest that he run the numbers together. In this code I LOVE YOU TRULY becomes 11-15-19-29-6-33-19-27-26-23-27-15-33.

Code 3: Each letter is represented by the shape of the enclosure it occupies in the unit below. If there is a dot above the complete unit, it is included with the code symbols in that unit.

A	B	C
D	E	F
G	H	I

J	K	L
M	N	O
P	Q	R

Thus, A is ⌐, B is ⊔, J is •⌐, and K is •⊔. I LOVE YOU TRULY is:

⌐ └• E ∧ ⊐ •< E •> ⌐• < L• <•

Invisible Writing. Onion juice, orange juice, sugar water, honey water, and soda pop are but some of the inks available. For onion ink, grate an onion to pulp and save the liquid that accumulates. Have your child use a toothpick as a pen and print in block letters. To make invisible writing visible, the message is held in the heat of a light bulb.

Mirror Writing. The great Leonardo da Vinci used mirror writing to describe his inventions. He wrote in a reverse script that progressed from right to left. For beginners, mirror printing may be easier. As a guide, the message is first put down as it ordinarily would be printed. Then it is printed with the words in reverse order with each word spelled backwards and with each letter reversed. The message MOUSE IN THE HOUSE!, for example, would read as follows:

!ƎƧUOH ƎHT NI ƎƧUOM

To decipher, the message is held to a mirror.

In another form of mirror writing the characters are printed upside down. Only the letter "S" needs to be reversed. In this form MOUSE IN THE HOUSE! would read

WOnƧE IN ⊥HE HOnƧEi

To decipher, a pocket or hand mirror is held at a right angle to the message.

Picture Writing. This also is known as rebus writing. The idea is to substitute pictures for individual words or groups of words. In a sense it is a step backwards since written language began with such symbols. However, rebus writing can be a vivid, charming method of communication. Consider this statement:

"The ☼ is shining and ✿ and 🐦 are everywhere."

It is as pleasant a way as I know of conveying the feeling of spring. Rebus writing will enliven a letter or a story a child has composed or a riddle he is trying on someone. If the symbols are sufficiently obscure, they also can serve as a code. Here is the beginning of a rebus vocabulary. Other symbols will occur to you and your youngster almost immediately.

- APPEAR
- COW
- BE
- COWBOY
- BEAUTIFUL
- BEE
- DELIGHT
- BEFORE
- EAR
- BEG
- EYE
- BEWARE
- BIRD
- FLIGHT

134 / THE RAINY DAY BOOK

FLOWER	🌸	START	☆T
FOUR	4	SUN	☀
HEAR	H👂	THEN	T🐔
HEN	🐔	TIE	👔
HOUSE	🏠	TIGHT	👔T
I	👁	TIME	👔M
MY	M👁	TINY	👔Z
ONE O'CLOCK	1⏰	TODAY	2 day
		TOMORROW	2 morrow
PAIR	🍐	WHEN	W🐔
SAW (VERB)	🪚	YOU	U

TOOTHPICK PUZZLES

Five to Four. Sixteen toothpicks are arranged as in the illustration so that they form five squares. The object is to reduce the five to four by moving three of the toothpicks to new positions.

Six to Two. Seventeen toothpicks are arranged in six squares. The six squares are to be reduced to two by *removing* six toothpicks, but leaving the others as they are.

Six to Three. The same arrangement of six squares is reduced to three by removing five toothpicks.

Eight to Five. Twenty-three toothpicks are arranged in eight squares. The eight are reduced to five by removing three toothpicks.

Nine to Two. Twenty-four toothpicks are arranged in nine squares. The nine are reduced to two by removing eight toothpicks.

Seven into Two. Form two squares with seven toothpicks.

11 ❀ Jokes, Riddles, Tongue Twisters

PLEASE understand that my children helped make the selections for this chapter. I tell you this not to escape responsibility but only to make clear what we have here. The jokes and riddles are particularly awful, which is why I think your children will enjoy them, too.

JOKES

First-Grader: My dad beats me up every morning.
Second-Grader: He does? How awful!
First-Grader: He gets up at six. I get up at seven.

Three boys were brought to the police station.
Captain, to the first boy: Why were you brought here?
First Boy: For throwing peanuts in the lake.
Captain, to the second boy: Why were you brought here?
Second Boy: For throwing peanuts in the lake.
Captain, to the third boy: Why are you here?
Third boy: I'm Peanuts.

Sam was invited to dinner at Johnny Smith's house.
Mrs. Smith: Sam, are you sure you can cut your meat?
Sam: Yes, Ma'am. We have meat this tough at home.

Father: You'd better drive more slowly. You're going eighty miles an hour.
Mother: Imagine that. And I only learned to drive yesterday.

Jokes, Riddles, Tongue Twisters / 137

John: May I have another cookie?
Mother: Another cookie, what?
John: Another cookie, please.
Mother: Please, what?
John: Please, Mother.
Mother: Please, Mother, what?
John: Please, Mother, dear.
Mother: No dear. You've already had too many.

Peter: If I scrub hard do you think I can get my face clean?
Mother: Let's soap for the best.

Father: Your report card says you failed everything but history. Why is that?
George: I don't take history.

Mother: John, there were two pieces of pie here last night. Now there is only one. Can you explain that?
John: It was so dark I didn't see the other piece.

David: Peanuts will make you fat.
John: How do you know?
David: Did you ever see a skinny elephant?

Peter: My big brother shaves every day!
Bobby: *My* brother shaves fifty times a day!
Peter: Is he crazy?
Bobby: No, he's a barber.

Man, to hotel clerk: I'd like a room and a bath, please.
Clerk: I can give you a room, sir, but you'll have to take your own bath.

Betsy: With which hand do you eat your mashed potatoes?
George: My right hand.
Betsy: *I* always use a fork.

Father: Did you use toothpaste?
Nancy: Why should I? None of my teeth are loose.

Mother: How are your marks at school?
Nancy: They are under water.
Mother: What do you mean?
Nancy: They are all below C level.

Lisa: Mother, will you change a dime for me?
Mother: Of course.
Lisa: Then change it into a quarter.

Peter: Can I borrow fifty cents?
Alan: I only have forty cents.
Peter: O.K. You can owe me a dime.

Peter: What did the jack say to the car?
John: Can I give you a lift?

Betsy: It's raining cars and dogs.
George: I know. I just stepped in a poodle.

Mother: This salad tastes terrible. Did you wash it?
Nancy: Yes. I not only used water, I used soap.

David: I don't deserve a zero for my mark.
Teacher: You are right, but I can't think of a lower mark to give you.

Father: Eat your spinach, son. It will give your cheeks color.
Son: But I don't want green cheeks.

George: Does your watch tell time?
Betsy: No. You have to look at it.

Teacher: Susan, spell the word "mouse."
Susan: M-o-u-s-
Teacher: And what's at the end?
Susan: A tail.

Sick Man: Doctor, help me. I think I am a dog.
Doctor: How long has this been going on?
Sick Man: Ever since I was a puppy.

John opened the refrigerator and found a squirrel inside.
John: What are you doing in our refrigerator?
Squirrel: Is this refrigerator a Westinghouse?
John: I think so.
Squirrel: I is westing.

Larry: What are you doing?
Peter: Writing a letter to my little brother.
Larry: But you haven't learned to write yet.
Peter: It doesn't matter. My brother hasn't learned to read yet.

RIDDLES

Why is a river rich?
It has two banks.

Why did the boy tiptoe past the medicine chest?
He didn't want to awaken the sleeping pills.

What did one wall say to the other wall?
Meet you at the corner.

Why does John keep running around his bed?
He wants to catch up on his sleep.

What did the big firecracker say to the little firecracker?
My pop is bigger than yours.

What is gray, has two ears, four legs, and a trunk?
A mouse going on vacation.

When is a boy most like a bear?
When he is barefooted.

Why did the boy throw the clock out the window a week before his birthday?
He wanted time to fly.

What has legs but cannot walk?
A table and a chair.

What goes OOM, OOM?
A cow walking backwards.

Why is a chicken on a fence like a coin?
Its head is one one side. Its tail is on the other.

Why does a cow go over a hill?
Because she can't get under it.

Why did the little house on the hill call a doctor?
It had panes in its windows.

Why is a lollipop like a race horse?
The faster you lick it, the faster it goes.

What nut is like a sneeze?
A cashew nut.

How many sides has a box?
Two. The inside and the outside.

Why does a baby pig eat so much?
To make a hog of himself.

What runs around all day and lies on the floor all night with its tongue hanging out?
A shoe.

What is the largest jewel in the world?
A baseball diamond.

What has 18 feet and catches flies?
A baseball team.

What runs, but never walks?
Water.

What did the mayonnaise say to the refrigerator?
Please close the door. I'm dressing.

Why do firemen wear red suspenders?
To hold up their pants.

Who was the fastest runner in history?
Adam. He was first in the human race.

What do hippopotamuses have that no other animals have?
Little hippopotamuses.

Why did the little drop of milk cry?
Because all his friends were in the jug.

What animal do you look like when you take a bath?
A little bear.

What does a sheep become after it is five years old?
Six years old.

Why was the little strawberry worried?
Because his father was in a jam.

In what month do people talk the least?
February. It's the shortest month.

What is the difference between "here" and "there"?
The letter "t."

What did the rug say to the floor?
Don't move! I've got you covered.

What time is it when the clock strikes thirteen?
Time to get the clock fixed.

Two men fell in the lake, but only one got his hair wet. Why?
The other was bald.

What insect needs the least food?
A moth. It lives on holes.

What runs from New York to Los Angeles without stopping?
A highway.

What has a head and a tail but no body?
A coin.

If you drop a rock into the Red Sea what does it become?
Wet.

What kind of a dog has no tail?
A hot dog.

What is big, blue, and eats boulders?
A big, blue boulder-eater.

What time is it when an elephant sits on a fence?
Time to get a new fence.

What kind of an animal jumps higher than a house?
All animals. Houses can't jump.

The more you add to it the smaller it becomes. The more you take away the larger it grows. What is it?
A hole.

Why did George drive his car over the cliff?
He wanted to try out his new air brakes.

A man was locked in a room with a piano. How did he get out?
He played until he found the right key.

Jokes, Riddles, Tongue Twisters / 143

Why were the Middle Ages called the Dark Ages?
Because there were so many knights then.

What kind of a dress do you have but never wear?
An address.

Why did Peter take a ruler to bed?
To see how long he slept.

Why do birds fly south?
It's too far to walk.

Why was the kangaroo cross with her children?
For eating crackers in bed.

Where does Friday come before Thursday?
In the dictionary.

Where was the Declaration of Independence signed?
At the bottom.

What has the head of a cat, the tail of a cat, yet isn't a cat?
A kitten.

What did Paul Revere say at the end of his famous ride?
Whoa!

TONGUE TWISTERS

Six thick thistle sticks.

How much dew could a dewdrop drop if a dewdrop could drop dew?

How many cans can a canner can
If a canner can can cans?
A canner can can as many cans as a canner can
If a canner can can cans.

Peter Piper picked a peck of pickled peppers.
Did Peter Piper pick a peck of pickled peppers?
If Peter Piper picked a peck of pickled peppers,
Where is the peck of pickled peppers Peter Piper picked?

She sells sea shells by the seashore.

Betty Botter bought some butter,
"But," she said, "this butter's bitter.
If I put it in my batter,
It will make my batter bitter.
But if I buy some better butter,
It will make my batter better."
So Betty bought some better butter,
Better than the bitter butter,
And she put it in the batter,
And it made the batter better.

Cross crossings cautiously.

Two tooters who tooted the flute
Tried to tutor two tutors to toot.
Said the two to the tutors,
"Is it harder to toot,
Or to tutor two tutors to toot?"

Bisquick—kiss quick.

Peter Prangle,
The prickly, prangly pear picker,
Picked three pecks of prangly, prickly pears,
From the prickly, prangly pear trees,
On the pleasant prairies.

Sam Slick saws six, slim, slippery, slender sticks.

Esaw Wood sawed wood. Esaw Wood saw wood. Oh, the wood that Wood would saw. One day Esaw Wood saw a saw saw wood as no other wood-saw Wood saw would saw wood. In fact, of all the wood-saws Wood ever saw

saw wood Wood never saw a wood-saw that would saw wood as the wood-saw Wood saw would.

How much wood would a wood chuck chuck if a wood chuck could chuck wood? He would chuck, he would, as much as he could, and chuck as much wood as a wood chuck would if a wood chuck could chuck wood.

The sun shines on the shop signs.

If to hoot and to toot a Hottentot tot be taught by a Hottentot tutor, should the tutor get hot if the Hottentot tot hoot and toot at the Hottentot tutor?

A big black bug bit a big black bear.

Susan shines shoes and socks. Shoes and socks shines Susan.

12 ❦ Music

Listening *Singing*
Making Rhythm Instruments

WHAT IS SUGGESTED in this chapter does not require talent or training or even the ability to carry a tune. All that is involved is singing songs you and your child like or listening to music you enjoy or perhaps making rhythm instruments and then singing or listening. The results may not always be melodious, but they are likely to soothe the soul.

LISTENING

Records are far more reliable than the radio in providing the kind of music you might like to hear at a particular time. If you visit the library for song books also borrow some records while you are there. The children's librarian may be an excellent source of advice on which ones your child might like. There also are several good lists to turn to. One is found in *The Complete Book of Children's Play* by Ruth Hartley and Robert Goldenson. Another is *Recordings for Children* by Augusta Baker, Ellin Greene, Spencer Shaw, and Mary Strang, which may be purchased for one dollar from the Office of Children's Services, New York Public Library, 20 West 53rd Street, New York, N. Y. 10019.

MAKING RHYTHM INSTRUMENTS

Pot covers, coffee cans, wooden spoons, and lamb chop bones all are potential music makers. So are kitchen forks, hatboxes, rubber bands, and many other things around the house one ordinarily does not associate with music. With little or no change, such objects readily become bells, gongs, drums, rattles, and other instruments children and parents can use in playing simple tunes, accompanying records, and experimenting with sound.

Bells. One of the smallest and pleasantest bell sounds can be obtained by suspending a fork from a string, then striking it with the handle of another fork or with a large nail. If it is the sound of sleighbells that is sought, jingle a bunch of keys or string some curtain rings together and jingle them. There also are two traditional approaches to consider. In one, small bells are stitched to a bracelet of elastic a child then wears. In the other, bells are stitched to a paper plate which is then used as a tambourine.

If there is interest in chimes, suspend a series of nails by string from a ruler or a stick and "play" them with another nail. Another traditional technique calls for eight drinking glasses containing different amounts of water. It is easy to fill and arrange them so they will reproduce the eight notes of the musical scale when tapped with a spoon or a pencil.

Cymbals and Gongs. For the crash of cymbals, bring two pot covers together. For the awe-inspiring sound of a gong, suspend a pot cover from a string and strike the cover with a wooden spoon. The heavier the cover the more gong-like will be the sound.

Drums. For an instant drum try a sturdy hatbox, which sounds somewhat like the tenor drum used in parades; a metal tray, which resembles a kettledrum in the sound it produces; or an empty, cylindrical oatmeal container, which sounds like a toy drum. If a full-fledged drum is what you have in mind, consider as a frame an empty coffee can, an old paint can, a salad bowl, or a nail keg. Cover the open end with heavy plastic, oilcloth, a tightly woven fabric such as Indianhead or denim, or a piece of rubber cut from an old rubber sheet or inner tube. Fasten the covering so that it is stretched taut. With a metal container use a large rubber band or a piece of wire to hold it in place. With a wooden container use thumbtacks. In this case first attach the covering to one side of the frame with one tack. Next pull the cover so that it is tight and insert another tack on the opposite side. Keeping the cover tightly drawn, then insert tacks every inch or two all the way around.

An unsharpened pencil makes a good drumstick. So does an empty thread spool in which a piece of doweling has been inserted as a handle. For a different kind of sound, brush the top of the drum with a whisk broom, a pastry brush, or a vegetable brush.

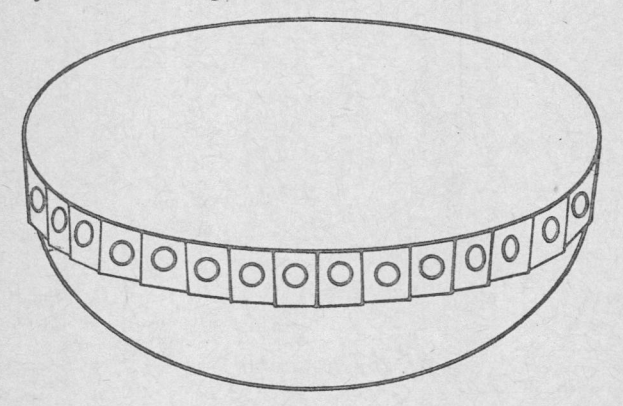

Rattles. The kind of container and what you put inside determine the sound. For a container, consider a paper bag; a spice, oatmeal, or salt box; a deflated balloon filled with rattling materials (see below), then inflated; or an empty can with a replaceable top such as a shoe polish or baking powder can. As noisemakers, try dried beans, rice grains, seeds, pebbles, sand, nails, buttons, jacks, bottle caps, or paper clips—in fact, any objects small enough to fit in the container and heavy enough to produce an audible sound.

If you happen to have a dried gourd, it makes an excellent rattle. If the seeds inside do not produce enough noise for your child, cut a hole in one end, add beans or pebbles, and seal the hole with tape. An unusual rattle also can be made with the small hoop-shaped bones in shoulder lamb chops. Scrub a half-dozen bones until they are clean, then dry them and arrange on a circlet of wire or string.

Rhythm Sticks and Blocks. Use these instruments to create rhythmic arrangements with a wooden quality. The handles of a wooden salad fork and salad spoon make excellent rhythm sticks. Grasping the bowl of the spoon in one hand and the prongs of the fork in the other, the musician rhythmically strikes one handle against the other. Two lengths of wood cut from an old broom handle or two pieces of medium-weight doweling also could be used as rhythm sticks.

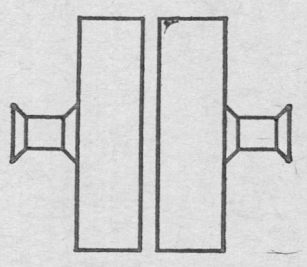

For rhythm blocks two rectangles of wood are needed. Pieces four inches by six inches by one-half inch are a good size. Nail an empty thread spool to each as a handle and clap the blocks together. For another kind of sound tack sandpaper to the undersides of the blocks, fastening it so that the paper wraps around the blocks and the tacks are on top. Then one block is rubbed against the other.

150 / THE RAINY DAY BOOK

Strings. For guitar-like rhythms, the player stretches four rubber bands over the length of an open cigar box, cheese box, or shoebox, or across the width of a large baking dish, and strums. For a banjo effect, he picks at the bands where they hug the bottom of the container. He also might play a series of rubber bands that have been stretched over the back of a chair. Still another possibility involves biting on one end of a rubber band, hooking the other end over a finger, and strumming with the other hand.

A homemade bass viol is another instrument to consider. It consists of an empty shoebox or a cylindrical container, two buttons, and a piece of string one to two feet long depending on the height of the child. A hole is punched in one end of the box. One end of the string is threaded through the hole and fastened to a button. Then the second button is tied to the other end of the string. To play this instrument the child sits on a chair and extends his legs. He places the box between his feet, holding the string taut with one hand, and plucks at it with the other.

Winds. A flute of sorts can be fashioned with a cardboard tube of the type paper towels are wrapped around.

Three or four small holes are punched in the top of the tube. One of the open ends is covered with a piece of waxed paper which is held in place with a rubber band. The musician hums into the other end, fingering the holes as with a flute or recorder. For music vaguely resembling that of a clarinet, flatten about one inch of the end of a drinking straw, then clip off the two corners. A sound is produced by blowing gently through this mouthpiece. Straws of different lengths yield different sounds.

If it is old-time kazoo music your child yearns for, have him fold a piece of waxed paper over a comb so that the comb's teeth rest in the fold. Next he places the folded end in his mouth with his lips barely touching the paper, then slowly moves the comb back and forth as he hums his favorite tune.

SINGING

Unless you have a fine memory you will need a few song books. Your library should have some of the following and others as well.

> *American Folk Songs for Children*, Ruth Crawford Seeger.
> *American Songbag*, Carl Sandburg.
> *Billy Boy*, Richard Chase. Drawings by Glen Rounds.
> *A Cat Came Fiddling and Other Rhymes of Childhood*, Paul Kapp.
> *Cock-a-Doodle-Do! Cock-a-Doodle-Dandy!* Paul Kapp.
> *The Fireside Book of Children's Songs*, Marie Winn.
> *Frog Went a' Courtin'*, John Langstaff. Illustrated by Feodor Rojankovsky.
> *Jean Ritchie's Swapping Song Book*, Jean Ritchie. Illustrated by George Pickow.
> *Lullabies and Night Songs*, Alec Wilder. Pictures by Maurice Sendak.

13 ❈ Storytelling

THE PLEASURES that lie in spending a rainy day with an intriguing book are well known. What a parent may overlook, however, is the equally agreeable experience of reading to a child. Part of the reward comes in having a responsive companion with whom to share an adventure. But there also is the opportunity through good stories to open doors to wonders and possibilities that are totally new to him.

The poet James Dickey wrote about this some years ago in terms of his experience with his children. "In the youngest," he observed, "one can see [developing] the gradual shy sense of the variousness and strangeness of the world. . . . For older children some of this lovely strangeness remains, but to it is added what the child has lived; the world for him is not so strange . . . it has lost the wonder of the unheard of . . . and picked up the equal wonder of potentiality: something that can and does happen, someplace I could go, someone I could meet."[1]

Librarians offer this advice on storytelling:

Read to a child as young as two, but be sure the story or poem is simple and the text has a strong rhythm.

When two children are separated by three or four years, read to the level of the oldest. When there is a greater age difference, read to each separately.

When there are a boy and a girl of school age in the audience, focus on stories boys prefer—which usually are

[1] "An Old Family Custom," *The New York Times Book Review*, June 6, 1965.

those that don't involve girls. (The girl won't mind; she also is intrigued by boys.)

Read only as long as the audience seems interested—perhaps ten minutes with the youngest children and a half hour with older ones.

Choose stories that appeal to you as well as to your audience.

The following list contains some 200 books selected by Ellin Greene, formerly the Storytelling Specialist at the New York Public Library. Your library undoubtedly has many of these books. For still other suggestions consult the children's librarian.

FOR THE YOUNGEST CHILDREN

ABC and COUNTING BOOKS
A Apple Pie, Kate Greenaway.
ABC Book, C. B. Falls.
ABC Bunny, Wanda Gag.
Brown Cow Farm; A Counting Book, Dahlov Ipcar.
Celestino Piatti's Animal ABC, Celestino Piatti.
Jeanne-Marie Counts Her Sheep, Françoise.
Over in the Meadow, John Langstaff.
Two Lonely Ducks, Roger Duvoisin.

MOTHER GOOSE

The Courtship, Merry Marriage, and the Feast of Cock Robin and Jenny Wren, to Which Is Added the Doleful Death of Cock Robin. Illustrated by Barbara Cooney.
Hey Diddle Diddle and Baby Bunting. Illustrated by Randolph Caldecott.
The Mother Goose Treasury. Illustrated by Raymond Briggs.
The Old Woman and Her Pig. Illustrated by Paul Galdone.
The Real Mother Goose. Illustrated by Blanche F. Wright.
Ring O' Roses. Illustrated by L. Leslie Brooke.

154 / THE RAINY DAY BOOK

PICTURE BOOKS

Andy and the Lion, James Daugherty.
Animal Babies, Ylla.
A Baby Sister for Frances, Russell Hoban.
Blueberries for Sal, Robert McCloskey.
A Boy Went Out To Gather Pears, Felix Hoffman.
Bruno Munari's Zoo, Bruno Munari.
Caps for Sale, Esphyr Slobodkina.
The Cock, the Mouse, and the Little Red Hen, Lecite Lefrevre.
Curious George, H. A. Rey.
Finders Keepers, Will and Nicolas.
Georgie, Robert Bright.
The Golden Goose Book, L. Leslie Brooke.
The Happy Lion, Louise Fatio.
Harry the Dirty Dog, Gene Zion.
Hide and Seek Fog, Alvin Tresselt.
I Had a Little . . . , Norma Levarie.
I Know a Lot of Things, Ann Rand.
In the Forest, Marie Hall Ets.
A Kiss is Round, Blossom Budney.
The Little Auto, Lois Lenski.
Little Blue and Little Yellow, Leo Lionni.
Little Tim and the Brave Sea Captain, Edward Ardizzone.
Little Toot, Hardie Gramatky.
Madeline, Ludwig Bemelmans.
Make Way for Ducklings, Robert McCloskey.
Mike Mulligan and His Steam Shovel, Virginia Lee Burton.
Millions of Cats, Wanda Gag.
The Mitten, Alvin Tresselt.
Mommy, Buy Me a China Doll, Harve and Margot Zemach.
Ola, Ingri and Edgar d'Aulaire.
Petunia, Roger Duvoisin.
Play With Me, Marie Hall Ets.
See the Circus, H. A. Rey.
Snowy Day, Ezra Jack Keats.

Storytelling / 155

The Speckled Hen, Harve and Margot Zemach.
The Story About Ping, Marjorie Flack.
The Story of Babar, Jean de Brunhoff.
The Story of Ferdinand, Munro Leaf.
The Tailor of Gloucester, Beatrix Potter.
The Tale of Peter Rabbit, Beatrix Potter.
The Three Billy Goats Gruff, Marcia Brown.
The Two Little Trains, Margaret Wise Brown.
The Umbrella, Taro Yashima.
Where the Wild Things Are, Maurice Sendak.
Whistle for Willie, Ezra Jack Keats.
White Snow, Bright Snow, Alvin Tresselt.
The Wolf and the Seven Little Kids, Felix Hoffman.

FOR CHILDREN FROM SIX TO TEN

Animal Stories and Nature

The Biggest Bear, Lynd Ward.
The Blind Colt, Glen Rounds.
Butterfly Time, Alice Goudey.
Chendu; the Boy and the Tiger, Astrid Sucksdorff.
Houses from the Sea, Alice Goudey.
King of the Wind, Marguerite Henry.
Rabbit Hill, Robert Lawson.
The Voyages of Doctor Dolittle, Hugh Lofting.

Family Stories

The Bears on Hemlock Mountain, Alice Dalgleish.
Blue Willow, Doris Gates.
Bright April, Marguerite de Angeli.
The Courage of Sarah Noble, Alice Dalgleish.
Crow Boy, Taro Yashima.
Gone-Away-Lake, Elizabeth Enright.
The Hundred Dresses, Eleanor Estes.
Impunity Jane, Rumer Godden.
In My Mother's House, Ann Nolan Clark.
Little House in the Big Woods, Laura Ingalls Wilder.
The Matchlock Gun, Walter D. Edmonds.

Maurice's Room, Paula Fox.
The Moffats, Eleanor Estes.
A Pocketful of Cricket, Rebecca Caudill.
Roller Skates, Ruth Sawyer.
A Street of Little Shops, Margery Bianco.
Time of Wonder, Robert McCloskey.
The Wheel on the School, Meindert de Jong.

Folk and Fairy Tales

Brer Rabbit, Joel Chandler Harris. Edited by Margaret Wise Brown.
Chanticleer and the Fox, Geoffrey Chaucer. Adapted and illustrated by Barbara Cooney.
Cinderella, Charles Perrault and Marcia Brown.
Down from the Lonely Mountain: California Indian Tales, Jane Louise Curry.
English Folk and Fairy Tales, Joseph Jacobs.
Favorite Fairy Tales Told in Czechoslovakia, Virginia Haviland.
The Giant Book, Beatrice Schenk de Regniers.
Hibernian Nights, Seumas MacManus.
Italian Peepshow, Eleanor Farjeon.
It's Perfectly True and Other Stories, Hans Christian Andersen.
The Jack Tales, edited by Richard Chase.
The Lost Half Hour, Eulalie Steinmetz Ross.
Puss In Boots, Charles Perrault and Marcia Brown.
Tales From Grimm, Wanda Gag.
Tales Told Again, Walter de la Mare.
The Talking Tree, Augusta Baker.
Terrapin's Pot of Sense, Harold Courlander.
The Tiger and the Rabbit and Other Puerto Rican Folk Tales, Pura Belpré.
The Ugly Duckling, Hans Christian Andersen. Edition illustrated by Johannes Larsen or Adrienne Adams.
The Wonder Clock, Howard Pyle.
Zlateh the Goat and Other Stories, Isaac Bashevis Singer.
Zomo the Rabbit, Hugh Sturton.

Storytelling / 157

FUNNY STORIES

Ben and Me, Robert Lawson.
The Five Chinese Brothers, Claire H. Bishop.
The Five Hundred Hats of Bartholomew Cubbins, Dr. Seuss.
Henry Huggins, Beverly Cleary.
Homer Price, Robert McCloskey.
Honk, the Moose, Phillip Stong.
Just So Stories, Rudyard Kipling.
Lentil, Robert McCloskey.
Mr. Popper's Penguins, Richard and Florence Atwater.
Mother Mother I Feel Sick Send for Doctor Quick Quick Quick, Remy Charlip and Burton Supree.
Peterkin Papers, Lucretia Hale.
The Three Policemen, William Pène du Bois.

FOR OLDER CHILDREN

ADVENTURE STORIES

The Adventures of Tom Sawyer, Mark Twain.
Banner in the Sky, James R. Ullman.
Big Tiger and Christian, Fritz Muhlenweg.
Call It Courage, Armstrong Sperry.
The Devil and Daniel Webster, Stephen Vincent Benét.
Ol' Paul, The Mighty Logger, Glen Rounds.
Onion John, Joseph Krumgold.
Pecos Bill, The Greatest Cowboy of All Times, James Cloyd Bowman.
The Pushcart War, Jean Merrill.
Rip Van Winkle and the Legend of Sleepy Hollow, Washington Irving.
Tales and Poems of Edgar Allan Poe, Edgar Allan Poe.
Tales of Sherlock Holmes, Arthur Conan Doyle.
Treasure Island, Robert Louis Stevenson.
The Twenty-one Balloons, William Pène du Bois.
A Wrinkle in Time, Madeleine L'Engle.

158 / The Rainy Day Book

Animal Stories and Nature

The Incredible Journey, Sheila Burnford.
The Jungle Books, Rudyard Kipling.
My Side of the Mountain, Jean George.
Old Yeller, Fred Gipson.
An Otter's Story, Emil Liers.
Owls in the Family, Farley Mowat.
Rain in the Woods and Other Small Matters, Glen Rounds.
Rascal, Sterling North.
Spring Comes to the Ocean, Jean George.
The Yearling, Marjorie Kinnan Rawlings.

Biography and Historical Fiction

Abe Lincoln Grows Up, Carl Sandburg.
Adam of the Road, Elizabeth Janet Gray.
Amos Fortune: Free Man, Elizabeth Yates.
Daniel Boone, James Daugherty.
The Door in the Wall, Marguerite de Angeli.
The Innocent Wayfaring, Marchette Chute.
Ishi, Last of His Tribe, Theodore Kroeber.
Island of the Blue Dolphins, Scott O'Dell.
Johnny Tremain, Esther Forbes.
Judith of France, Margaret Leighton.
Tituba of Salem Village, Ann Petry.
The Trumpeter of Krakow, Eric P. Kelly.
Warrior Scarlet, Rosemary Sutcliff.
The Witch of Blackbird Pond, Elizabeth Speare.

Tales of Heroes, Tall Tales, Legends

The Adventures of Odysseus and the Tale of Troy, Padraic Colum.
The Adventures of Rama, Joseph Gaer.
Children of Odin, Padraic Colum.
Heroes of the Kalevala, Babette Deutsch.
The Merry Adventures of Robin Hood, Howard Pyle.
Never to Die: The Egyptians in Their Own Words, Josephine Mayer and Tom Prideaux.

Stories from the Bible, Walter de la Mare.
The Story of King Arthur and His Knights, Howard Pyle.
A Taste of Chaucer, Selections from the Canterbury Tales, edicted by Anne Malcolmson.
Thunder of the Gods, Dorothy Hosford.

FANTASY FOR ALL AGES

The Adventures of Pinocchio, C. Collodi.
Alice's Adventures in Wonderland and *Through the Looking Glass,* Lewis Carroll. Illustrated by Tenniel.
The Animal Family, Randall Jarrell.
The Bee-Man of Orn, Frank Stockton and Maurice Sendak.
The Borrowers, Mary Norton.
The Cat Who Went to Heaven, Elizabeth Coatsworth.
The Children of Green Knowe, Lucy M. Boston.
The Hobbit, J. R. R. Tolkein.
The Lion, the Witch, and the Wardrobe, C. S. Lewis.
The Little Bookroom: Eleanor Farjeon's Short Stories for Children.
The Little Prince, Antoine de Saint-Éxupéry.
The Magic Pictures, Marcel Ayme.
Mary Poppins, P. L. Travers.
Miss Hickory, Carolyn Bailey.
My Father's Dragon, Ruth Stiles Gannett.
Peter Pan, James Barrie.
The Return of the Twelves, Pauline Clarke.
Rootabaga Stories, Carl Sandburg.
Stuart Little, E. B. White.
The Wind in the Willows, Kenneth Grahame.
Winnie-the-Pooh, A. A. Milne.
The Wizard of Oz, L. Frank Baum and W. W. Denslow.

POETRY FOR ALL AGES

The Birds and the Beasts Were There, William Cole.
A Book of Nonsense, Edward Lear.

160 / THE RAINY DAY BOOK

Come Hither, Walter de la Mare.
Early Moon, Carl Sandburg.
Eleanor Farjeon's Poems for Children, Eleanor Farjeon.
Golden Slippers, Arna Bontemps.
Imagination's Other Place, Poems of Science and Mathematics, Helen Plotz.
Lean Out of the Window, Sara Hannum and Gwendolyn E. Reed.
A Little Laughter, Katherine Love.
Miracles: Poems by Children of the English-Speaking World, Richard Lewis.
The Moment of Wonder: A Collection of Chinese and Japanese Poetry, Richard Lewis.
The Pied Piper of Hamelin, Robert Browning. Illustrated by Kate Greenaway.
Poems Selected for Young People, Edna St. Vincent Millay.
Poems for Youth, Emily Dickinson.
Rhymes and Verses, Walter de la Mare.
A Rocket in My Pocket. The Rhymes and Chants of Young Americans, Carl Withers.
This Way, Delight, Herbert Read.
When We Were Very Young, Now We Are Six, A. A. Milne.
You Come Too, Robert Frost.
Yours Till Niagara Falls, Lillian Morrison.

14 ❧ Good Things to Eat

Kitchen Projects   *Candy Recipes*

KITCHEN PROJECTS

SOME OF THE MOST PLEASANT HOURS I have spent with my children have been in the kitchen making good things to eat. The warmth of the room, the nice smells, the pleasure that comes from creating something other people will enjoy yield a kind of brightness that often is hard to capture even when the sun is shining. No matter what the project, a child as young as three or four can make some contribution, be it tearing lettuce leaves, washing vegetables, or helping to ice a cake. If he has reached seven or eight, there are many things he can prepare pretty much on his own, such as puddings and gelatins from mixes, sandwiches, salad dressings, and even scrambled eggs.

Something our children particularly enjoy is helping to plan and prepare meals. It may be a rainy day lunch which they then eat on the living room floor as if at a picnic, or it might be a dinner party to mark Father's return from toil or some other significant event. Planning a menu for such a celebration, obtaining the ingredients (which might mean a trip to the grocer's or a neighbor's), preparing the meal itself, and creating decorations and party hats (see Chapter 2: Paper, and Chapter 3: Hats) has occupied them on occasion for much of a day.

Something else they like is making candy. Perhaps

your child would enjoy that, too. Here are a dozen old-fashioned candy recipes to consider.

CHOCOLATE DROPS

8 *ounces semisweet chocolate*
½ *teaspoon vanilla*
1 *cup nutmeats in small pieces*
or 1 *cup raisins*

Melt the chocolate in the top of a double boiler. Remove from the heat, add the vanilla and the nutmeats or raisins, and blend well. Drop teaspoonfuls of the mixture on a cookie sheet covered with waxed paper and chill until firm. If bitter chocolate is used, add one cup of granulated sugar after the chocolate has melted but before the other ingredients are included.

FONDANT

1 *egg white*
1 *tablespoon water*
1 *tablespoon evaporated milk*
½ *teaspoon vanilla*
2½ *cups confectioners' sugar*
food coloring (optional)
raisins, nutmeats, or other fillings (optional)

Beat together the egg white, water, milk, and vanilla. Next, slowly add the sugar, blending thoroughly, and knead until the mixture is smooth. If the fondant seems sticky, add more sugar. If it seems too dry, add more milk or water. Then add food coloring and the raisins, nutmeats, or other fillings. Cover and refrigerate until firm.

FUDGE

5 *squares semisweet chocolate*
One 4¼ *-ounce chocolate bar in pieces*
⅔ *cup marshmallow cream*
1 *tablespoon butter*
1½ *cups nutmeats or raisins (optional)*
⅔ *cup light cream or evaporated milk*
1½ *cups granulated sugar*

Melt chocolate squares and chocolate bar. Combine the first four ingredients in a bowl with the nutmeats or raisins. Blend the cream and sugar in a saucepan and boil for 5 minutes, stirring throughout. Add to the ingredients in the bowl and mix until smooth. Then empty into an ungreased pan, cool, and cut into squares.

GUMDROPS

These also go by the name of Turkish Delight. A child must wait until the next day to eat them but in this case waiting is worthwhile.

2 tablespoons unflavored gelatin	1½ cups granulated sugar
½ cup cold water	⅛ teaspoon salt
¾ cup fruit juice	1 tablespoon lemon juice
	1 teaspoon vanilla

Soak the gelatin in the water. Add the fruit juice, sugar, and salt to a saucepan, stirring until the sugar is dissolved. Then add the gelatin and boil for 15 minutes. Remove from the heat, add the lemon juice and vanilla, pour into a wet pan, and chill overnight. The next day cut into pieces with a warm knife and roll in sugar.

ROCK CANDY

This also is known as crystal candy since it consists of sugar crystals.

1 lollipop stick or pencil
1 clean 6-inch length of string
1 paper clip
½ cup water
granulated sugar

Arrange the stick, string, and clip in a glass jar or tumbler as shown in the illustration. Add the water to a saucepan and bring to a boil. Next add the sugar teaspoon by teaspoon until no more will dissolve. Pour the solution into the jar and set uncovered in a warm place where it will not be disturbed. Within a few days sugar crystals should begin to form on the string. Within a week or two they may be large enough to qualify as candy.

SOMEMORES

This is a gooey confection concocted by the Girl Scouts of America.

BASIC SOMEMORE
1 *marshmallow*
2 *pieces of milk chocolate*
2 *graham crackers*

Toast the marshmallow. Place it between the two pieces of chocolate; then place the chocolate between the two graham crackers.

VARIATIONS
Use apple slices instead of graham crackers.
Use peanut butter, chocolate-covered peppermints, or chocolate-covered graham crackers instead of the chocolate.

The following recipes require a candy thermometer.

CANDIED APPLES

2 *cups brown sugar*
⅔ *cup water*
1 *tablespoon light corn syrup*
½ *teaspoon lemon juice*
lollipop or popsicle sticks
apples
1 *bowl ice water*

Place the first three ingredients in a saucepan. Stir until the sugar dissolves, then boil until a candy thermometer registers 290 degrees. Remove from the heat and add the lemon juice. Insert sticks in the apples, dip the apples in the syrup, and plunge them into the ice water. Place on a greased cookie sheet to dry.

DIVINITY

2 egg whites
2 cups granulated sugar
½ cup light corn syrup
½ cup water
1 teaspoon vanilla
1 cup nutmeats, raisins, or candied fruit (optional)

Beat the egg whites until stiff. Add the sugar, syrup, and water to a saucepan, stirring until the sugar is dissolved. Then boil until candy thermometer registers 250 to 265 degrees. Remove from the heat and pour over the egg whites. Next beat the mixture with an electric mixer until it is stiff and has lost its glossy quality. This usually takes about 15 minutes. Finally, add the vanilla, and the nutmeats, raisins, or candied fruit. Pour into a greased pan and cut into squares.

PEANUT BRITTLE

½ cup granulated sugar
½ cup brown sugar
½ cup light corn syrup
¼ cup cold water
1½ cups roasted peanuts
1 teaspoon baking soda
1 tablespoon butter
1 teaspoon vanilla

Blend the sugar, syrup, and water, stirring until the sugar is dissolved. Add the peanuts and boil to 244 degrees. Remove from the heat, add the remaining ingredients, and stir rapidly. Then immediately pour onto a greased cookie sheet. After the brittle has hardened, break it into pieces.

LEATHER APRONS

This is an old Vermont recipe which requires a snowy day or at least some fresh snow on the ground.

1 cup pure maple syrup or:	½ cup granulated sugar
¾ cup light corn syrup	snow
¼ cup pancake syrup mixture	doughnuts (optional)
	pickles (optional)

When we don't have pure maple syrup, my wife uses a mixture of corn syrup, pancake syrup, and sugar, which she stirs until the sugar is dissolved. Boil either the pure syrup or the mixture to 238 degrees. Then send your youngster out for a pan of clean snow. Pour the hot syrup on the snow a small quantity at a time. Each pouring will yield a candy the color and perhaps the shape of a leather apron. If your youngster wears braces on his teeth, advise him to suck rather than chew. Vermonters traditionally eat dougnuts with these candies to blot up the stickiness. They also eat pickles to cut the sweetness.

POPCORN BALLS

1 cup granulated sugar	¼ teaspoon salt
⅓ cup water	½ teaspoon vanilla
1 tablespoon butter	½ teaspoon vinegar
3 tablespoons light corn syrup	2 quarts popped corn

Place the sugar, water, butter, and corn syrup in a saucepan and stir until the sugar is dissolved. Boil to 248 degrees. Add the salt, vanilla, and vinegar and continue boiling to 290 degrees. Then pour the syrup slowly over the popped corn, distributing it with a wooden spoon. Next coat your hands and your child's with butter, shape the popcorn into balls, and place them on a greased cookie sheet to harden.

TAFFY

This is the messiest recipe in this chapter, but it also is the most fun.

1½ cups light molasses	⅛ teaspoon salt
2 teaspoons vinegar	1½ tablespoons butter
½ cup granulated sugar	

Add the molasses, vinegar, and sugar to a large saucepan. Stir over low heat until the sugar is dissolved. Next turn the heat up to medium and boil until the thermometer registers 240 degrees. Then add the salt and butter and continue boiling to 265 degrees. Pour the mixture onto a greased cookie sheet. While it cools, coat your hands and your child's with butter. Then pull and stretch the taffy until it is soft and chewy. Finally, cut it into 1-inch pieces and wrap those you don't eat right away in waxed paper.

15 ❧ Letting Off Steam

Active Games *Housework*
Exercises *Loud Noises*

ONE OF THE COMMON PROBLEMS of a rainy day is that a child has far more energy than he can use and gets far less exercise than he needs. As a result, after a while he may become restless and hard to manage. It is at such times that the activities in this chapter may be helpful. Most give a child a chance to use the muscles he would use if he were running and playing outdoors. Some also encourage him to make noise. This isn't exercise exactly, but it helps him to let off steam.

ACTIVE GAMES

Action. Two players face one another. If there are more than two they form a circle. The first player makes a movement of some sort, such as jumping, waving, or clapping. The second repeats this movement and adds one of his own. Then each player in turn repeats the earlier movements and contributes a new one. If a player forgets a movement or repeats it in the wrong order, he drops out of the game. The last player left is the winner.

Balloon Ball. A piece of string is extended between two chairs. The players take positions on either side of the string as in a game of volleyball. They then hit the ball back and forth over the string with their hands, scoring a point each time the opposing player fails to make a return. The winner of one round serves the ball in the next round. The first to score twenty-one points wins the game.

Basement Play. There are at least four activities that may be practical: jumping rope, roller skating, hopscotch, and shuffleboard. For the latter two, outline the playing area in chalk. For shuffleboard, use pot covers and brooms.

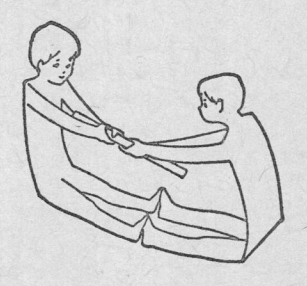

Big Stick. Two evenly matched children and a broomstick are needed. The youngsters sit on the floor facing one another with legs extended and the soles of their feet pressed against those of their opponent. They both grasp the stick, holding it a short distance above their toes. At a signal each pulls as hard as he can, trying to bring the other to his feet or cause him to roll over on his side or drop the stick.

Chicken Fight. Two players are involved. Each stands on one leg with his arms folded across his chest. His objective is to hop to his opponent, bump him hard, and make him lose his balance.

Dancing. This is not dancing in the accepted sense. It is instead a free response to music. Ballet music is good for this purpose; so is band music. First have your child take off his shoes so that he can dance in his stocking feet. Then encourage him to move as the music suggests. If the music whirls or falls or rises, so might he. If it clomps like a horse in a meadow or glides like a boat on a quiet lake or circles madly like a carousel, so might he.

Finger Bend. Two players face one another, raise their arms overhead, and grasp their opponent's hands, interweaving their fingers. Without releasing their hands, they bring their arms down and take one step back. From this position each attempts to force the other to kneel.

**Finger Tips.* A child attempts to touch the fingertips of one hand to the wrist just above.

Hand Push. Two players stand toe to toe, their palms pressed against their opponent's palms at chest level. At a signal, each pushes as hard as he can. The first one to force the other to step back is the winner of that round.

Hide and Seek. The object is, of course, for the player who is It to hide so well somewhere in the house that those who seek him cannot find him.

**Pick Up.* A youngster picks up a handkerchief, washcloth, or towel from the floor using only his toes.

Simon Says. One player is Simon. The other players do what he asks if he precedes his request with the expression "Simon Says"—for example, "Simon says do five pushups." If he makes his request without the preface "Simon Says," the players do nothing. If a player does what he asks under such circumstances, he pays a forfeit which Simon decides.

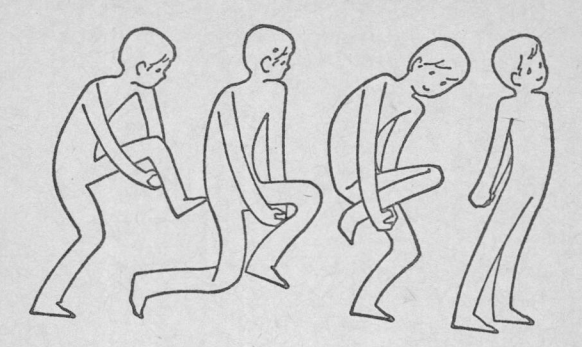

Step Through. A youngster clasps his hands in a loop in front of him. He pulls one leg through the loop and then the other.

Stepping Stones. Pieces of paper representing stones are arranged around a room in the form of a path, with some pieces close together and others far apart. The player attempts to step from one "stone" to the next, placing only one foot on each as he moves along. If he walks the path successfully in this way, ask him to do it again—this time with a book balanced on his head.

Wastepaper Basket. A child places a wastepaper basket against a wall. He steps back from the basket, leans forward, and presses his forehead against the wall. He then lifts the basket from the floor and tries to stand upright. He will find, however, that he cannot, no matter how hard he tries.

Weighing. Two youngsters stand back to back and link their arms. One bends forward and lifts the other from the floor, using his back as a lever. When the other player regains his feet, he lifts his comrade from the floor. They continue in this fashion until they've had enough.

EXERCISES

The exercises described in this section are part of a physical fitness program developed by the Royal Canadian Air Force for its staff and their families. What makes these exercises more interesting than most is that they are organized by levels of achievement toward which the exerciser works. Starting the program on one rainy day and doing the exercises daily thereafter, by the next rainy day a child may have moved to a considerably higher level of achievement. The set of five suggested should take a healthy youngster of six about fifteen minutes to complete.

Exercise 1. The exerciser stands with his feet apart and arms raised. He bends and attempts to touch the floor. Then he stretches his arms upward and backward, arching his back slightly.

Exercise 2. The exerciser lies on his back with his feet six inches apart and his arms at his sides. Keeping his legs

Letting Off Steam / 173

straight, he raises his head and shoulders just enough to see his heels, then returns to the starting position.

Exercise 3. He now lies on the floor front down, his palms placed under his thighs. He raises his head and also one leg, which he keeps straight at the knee. As the exercise is repeated, the legs are used alternately.

Exercise 4. This exercise resembles a pushup. The exerciser lies front down with his hands positioned under his shoulders and his palms flat on the floor. He then straightens his arms. In doing so he raises the upper part of his body but keeps his knees on the floor. He then returns to his starting position.

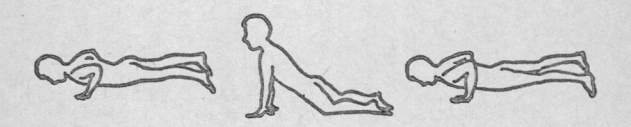

Exercise 5. The exerciser runs in place. Each time he completes seventy-five steps he does ten scissors jumps, then continues running. A scissor jump involves standing with the right leg and left arm extended forward and the left leg and right arm extended backward, then jumping and reversing these positions before landing.

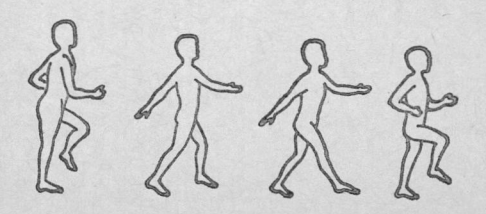

The progress chart used with these exercises is shown below. The exerciser starts at D —. The day after he has mastered this level, he progresses to the next. The levels

Level	\multicolumn{5}{c}{EXERCISE}
	1	2	3	4	5
A+	20	18	22	13	400
A	18	17	20	12	375
A−	16	15	18	11	335
B+	14	13	16	9	320
B	12	12	14	8	305
B−	10	11	12	7	280
C+	8	9	10	6	260
C	7	8	9	5	235
C−	6	7	8	4	205
D+	4	5	6	3	175
D	3	4	5	3	145
D−	2	3	4	2	100
Minutes for each exercise	2	1	1	1	6

must be taken in order. A youngster of six ultimately may be able to achieve Level B. A youngster of seven eventually may reach Level A. However, it is recommended that they do not go beyond these levels until they are older. Children above seven should set their sights for A. When they are ready for more advanced exercises, consult the *Royal Canadian Air Force Exercise Plans for Physical Fitness,* published in paperback for one dollar by Simon & Schuster, Inc.[1]

[1] The exercises and illustrations used here are adapted from this book with the permission of *This Week* Magazine.

HOUSEWORK

Household chores also are an excellent source of exercise for a child. Furthermore, most children like housework. Here are some possibilities:

Destroying cobwebs
Dusting
Rearranging furniture, particularly in the child's room
Sorting and folding laundry
Vacuuming
Washing bathtubs, shower stalls, sinks
Washing dishes
Washing insides of windows
Washing the kitchen floor
Washing smudges off walls
Washing woodwork

Rather than assign your child a task, give him this list and let him make his own choice. It will seem less like work and more like fun. However, also be realistic about what he can achieve.

LOUD NOISES

The occasional opportunity to make a loud noise, as loud as one wishes, offers satisfactions that should not be underestimated. Here are two ear-shattering possibilities. One involves a balloon into which a child blows and blows until it explodes. The other is the traditional paper bag explosion. A youngster fills a bag with air, twists the opening closed, then claps his hand against the bag —hard! For other ideas, see Chapter 12.

16 ❀ Excursions in the Rain

OF COURSE, you don't *have* to stay home all day just because the weather is bad. You could take your child out to lunch or buy him a treat or visit some shops that would interest him. You also might take a walk in the rain or go to the movies or visit any one of dozens of intriguing places nearby. One of the nice things about a rainy day excursion, in fact, is that many people are at home and most places you might want to visit are uncrowded. Unless lunch is involved, plan your trip for the early afternoon, a time when you and your child both might be ready for a change of scenery. Consider these possibilities:

Aquarium, Zoo. Be there at feeding time if possible.

Dairy Farm. Visit the one which provides your milk. First check with your milkman or call the company involved.

Factory. A tour might be of interest to children of at least eight. Plants where candy is made, bread is baked, food is processed, and cars or aircraft are assembled often are the most popular. However, not all firms welcome visitors. First call the public relations or personnel office.

Father. The idea is to see him at work and learn something about where he works. If such a visit is feasible, arrange things in advance and don't stay too long.

Fire House, Police Station. Sitting in the cab of a fire truck is one attraction. Standing in an empty jail cell is, for some reason, another. Telephone first to be certain there isn't an emergency in progress.

Greenhouse. If your child is indifferent to flowers, the curious sight and sound of rain beating down on an enormous glass roof may appeal to him.

Library. One objective might be acquiring a pile of books and records to take home. Another might be finding out just how the library works. If the librarian isn't too busy, perhaps she could show you around.

Museum. Children of school age are likely to enjoy themselves. If this is to be a first visit, call the museum's education office for advice on which exhibits might be most appropriate.

Newspaper. Try to arrange a tour when the presses are rolling.

Parks, Woods. A walk in the rain through a park or the woods can be delightful if you are dressed for the weather and if you take time to look around. For example, are there birds and animals to be seen? Are there insects about? Are the sounds and colors different from when the weather is fair?

Shops. Department stores, hardware stores, music shops, and pet shops offer good browsing. Others may be of interest for the techniques used. If your butcher, baker, cobbler, or fishmonger isn't busy, perhaps he would let your youngster see what it is like backstage.

Transportation. A brief journey by train or bus might appeal to a younger child.

Weather Bureau. If a visit can be arranged, this is a fascinating place to tour when the weather is bad. For one thing, you learn about forecasting; for another, you learn when the sun is expected to shine again. You might find that tomorrow is the day.

17 ❧ Solutions to Puzzles

CHAPTER 2

Words and Letters

House to Mouse
East to west: east—past—pest—west
Heat to cold: heat—head—held—hold—cold
Walk to ride: Walk—talk—tale—tile—tide—ride

States and Capitals

Alabama—Montgomery
Alaska—Juneau
Arizona—Phoenix
Arkansas—Little Rock
California—Sacramento
Colorado—Denver
Connecticut—Hartford
Delaware—Dover
Florida—Tallahassee
Georgia—Atlanta
Hawaii—Honolulu
Idaho—Boise
Illinois—Springfield
Indiana—Indianapolis
Iowa—Des Moines
Kansas—Topeka
Kentucky—Frankfort
Louisiana—Baton Rouge
Maine—Augusta
Maryland—Annapolis
Massachusetts—Boston
Michigan—Lansing
Minnesota—Saint Paul
Mississippi—Jackson
Missouri—Jefferson City

Montana—Helena
Nebraska—Lincoln
Nevada—Carson City
New Hampshire—Concord
New Jersey—Trenton
New Mexico—Santa Fe
New York—Albany
North Carolina—Raleigh
North Dakota—Bismarck
Ohio—Columbus
Oklahoma—Oklahoma City
Oregon—Salem
Pennsylvania—Harrisburg
Rhode Island—Providence
South Carolina—Columbia
South Dakota—Pierre
Tennessee—Nashville
Texas—Austin
Utah—Salt Lake City
Vermont—Montpelier
Virginia—Richmond
Washington—Olympia
West Virginia—Charleston
Wisconsin—Madison
Wyoming—Cheyenne

Wrrrrrr

wager	weaker	whichever	widower
waiter	wear	whimper	winder
walker	weather	whipper-	winner
wallflower	weaver	snapper	winter
wallpaper	weeper	whir	wiper
wander	Westerner	whisker	wither
wanderer	whaler	whisper	wonder
war	whatever	whistler	worker
warbler	whenever	whoever	wrapper
washer	wherever	whopper	wringer
water	whether	wicker	writer
		wider	

CHAPTER 11

Checker Puzzles
Lineup

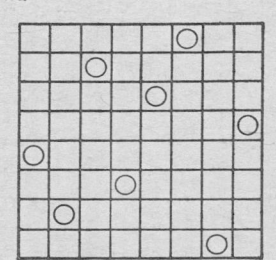

Middleman — 1, 2, 3, 4; the bottom checker from stack 1 slides out to position 4.

Number Puzzles
Magic Squares

7	2	6
4	5	6
4	8	3

8	6	7
6	7	8
7	8	6

In both squares other solutions also are possible.

180 / The Rainy Day Book

Missing Numbers

Addition	Subtraction	Multiplication
302	710	920
663	124	41
702	586	920
1667		3680
		37720

Paper and Pencil Puzzles
Don't Lift the Pencil

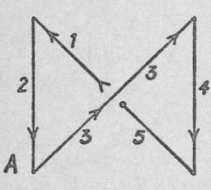

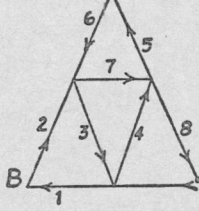

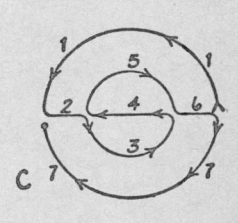

Lines
Three-Line Puzzle

Six-Line Puzzle

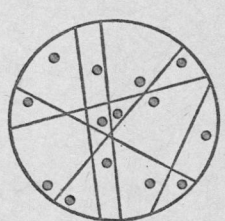

Toothpick Puzzles
Five to Four

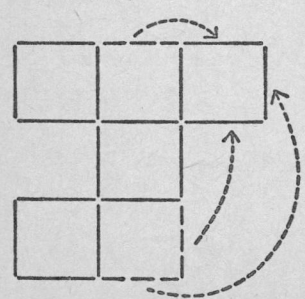

Six to Two

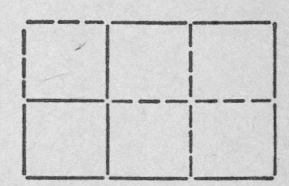

Solutions to Puzzles / 181

Six to Three

Eight to Five

Seven into Two

Nine to Two

Index

Accuracy (button game), 18
Action (action game), 168
Air, Earth, Water (word and letter game), 46
Airplanes:
  clothespin, 59
  paper, 65-66
Alphabet (magazine game), 32
Anagrams (word and letter game), 46-47
Around the Clock (playing card game), 39-40
Arts and crafts, 51-81
Asterisk designation, 13
Attics, 100-01

Balance (book game), 18
Ball games, 16-17
  Blow Ball, 16
  Bouncing, 16
  Bowling, 16-17
  Catch, 17
  Golf, 17
Balloon Ball (game), 168-69
Balloon games, 15-16
  Basketball, 15
  Release, 16
  Strike, 16
Bank (making), 52
Baseball (button game), 19
Basements, 100-01, 169

Basketball:
  balloon game, 15
  button game, 20
Basket (making), 53
Baths, 99
Beads (making), 57-58
Bean games, 17-18
  Hul Gul, 17
  Odd-Even, 18
  Ping, 18
Bells, 147
Belts (making), 56
Between the Scissors (checker game), 25-26
Blow Ball (ball game), 16
Boats (making):
  bottle caps, 52
  box, 53
  paper, 66
  soap, 76
Bookends (making), 81
Books, 151-60
  ABC, 153
  adventure stories, 157-58
  animal stories, 155, 158
  biography, 158
  counting, 153
  fairy tales, 156
  family stories, 155-56
  fantasy for all ages, 159
  folk tales, 156

for children six to ten, 155-57
for older children, 157-59
for youngest children, 153-55
funny stories, 157
hero stories, 158-59
historical fiction, 158
legends, 158-59
Mother Goose, 153
nature stories, 155, 158
picture books, 154-55
poetry for all ages, 159-60
song, 151
tall tales, 158-59
Bottle cap arts and crafts, 52
boat, 52
top, 52
Bouncing (ball game), 16
Bowling (ball game), 16-17
Bowls (making), 58
Box arts and crafts, 52-56
bank, 52
basket, 53
boat, 53
bridge, 53
castle, 53
cave, 53
cradle, 53-54
furniture for doll house, 54
peep shows, 54-55
roller toy, 55
train, 55-56
tunnel, 53
Box games:
Button Box, 21
Catch, 17
Quoits, 28
Roll-Away, 32
Bread board (making), 81
Bridges (making), 53
Bubbles, 96-97
Button arts and crafts, 56-57
belt, 56
crown, 56
earrings, 56
necklace, 56
pictures, 56
Whirligig, 57
Button Box (quiet game), 21
Button games, 18-24
Accuracy, 18
Baseball, 19
Basketball, 20-21
Button Box, 21
Guessing, 21
Mill, 21-22
Odd-Even, 18
Snap, 23
Sunshine and Rain, 24-25
Tick Tack Toe, 23
Toss, 23-24

Calendar games, 24-25
Sunshine and Rain, 24-25
Toss, 24
California (memory game), 33
Candy, recipes for, 161-67
Candied Apples, 164-65
Chocolate Drops, 162
Divinity, 165
Fondant, 162
Fudge, 162-63
Gumdrops, 163
Leather Aprons, 166
Peanut Brittle, 165
Popcorn Balls, 166
Rock Candy, 163-64
Somemores, 164
Taffy, 167
Turkish Delight, 163
Canoes (making), 66
Capital Cities (checker game), 26
Capitals of states, list of, 178
Cards *see* Playing card activities
Cartons for dramatic play, 82-83
Castles (making), 53

INDEX / 185

Casts, leaf, 114-15
Catch (ball game), 17
Categories *see* Guggenheim
Caves (making), 53
Chains (making), 67
Checkers:
   Between the Scissors, 25-26
   Capital Cities, 26
   Five in a Line, 26
   Football, 26-27
   Fox and Geese, 27
   Kings, 28
   puzzles, 125-26
Chew Fast (candy game), 25
Chicken Fight (action game), 169
Clay arts and crafts, 57-58
   beads, 57-58
   bowls, 58
Closets, 100-01
Cloth arts and crafts:
   belts, 56
   curtains for doll house, 58
   pictures, 56
   samplers, 58
Clothes *see* Costumes
Clothespin arts and crafts:
   airplanes, 59
   dolls, 85
Clothespin games:
   Bowling, 16-17
   Dropping, 28
   Fishing, 98
   Quoits, 28
Codes *see* Secret Writing
Coin arts and crafts, 59
   rubbings, 59
Collages, 59
Collections, 103
Container Toss (button game), 24
Contents (memory game), 33
Cooking, 161-67

Cootie (dice game), 29
Costumes:
   boots, 83
   chemise, 84
   coats, 84
   collars, 84
   crowns, 56, 88
   gauntlets, 85
   gloves, 85
   hats, 87-89
   headdress, Indian, 68
   helmet, 88
   muffs, 85
   shirts, 85
   ties, 84
   vests, 85
Counters *see* Button games
Cradles (making), 53-54
Crafts, 51-81
Crayon arts and crafts:
   Animals, 59
   Defacement, 59-60
   Dots, 60
   Dots and Lines, 60
   Double Drawing, 60
   Drawing in the Dark, 60
   leaf prints, 115
   rubbings, 59
   Shadow Drawing, 60-61
   tracings, 61
Croquet (thread spool game), 45
Cup-a-phone (making), 72-73
Cup Stick Game (paper cup game), 34-35
Cut-outs, 67
Cymbals, 147

Dancing, 169-70
Designs:
   string, 77
   yarn, 77
Diaries, 108

186 / INDEX

Dice games, 29-30
  Cootie, 29
  Elimination, 29
  Steeplechase, 29-30
Diorama (making), 54
Dolls for dramatic play, 85-87
Don't Lift the Pencil (puzzle), 129-30
Dots and Lines (paper and pencil game), 35
Double Numbers (paper and pencil game), 35-36
Dramatic play, 82-95
  blankets, 83
  cartons, 82-83
  costumes, 83-85
  dolls, 85-87
  makeup, 89
  masks, 90
  puppets, 91-93
  puppet theaters, 93-94
  shadows, 94-95
  sheets, 83
Drawers, 100-01
Drawing *see* Crayon arts and crafts
Drinking straw arts and crafts, 61
  jewelry, 61
  Straw Ball, 61
Drinking straw games:
  Croquet, 45
  Pick Up, 30
  Ping, 18
Drop It (identification game), 31
Dropping (clothespin game), 28
Drums, 147-48

Earrings (making), 56
Eleven Up (question game), 43
Elimination (dice game), 29
Envelope arts and crafts, 61
  bracelets, 61

Excursions, 176-77
  aquarium, 176
  bus, 177
  dairy farm, 176
  factory, 176
  fire house, 176-77
  greenhouse, 177
  library, 177
  museum, 177
  newspaper office, 177
  park, 177
  police station, 176-77
  shop, 177
  train, 177
  visit father at work, 176
  weather bureau, 177
  woods, 177
Exercises, 172-74
Experiments, science, 118-24
Eyeglasses, wire, 80

Fabric scraps for costumes, 83
Faces:
  makeup, 89
  masks, 90
  paper, 68
Feel the Raisin (identification game), 31
Figures:
  pipe cleaner, 87
  potato, 87
  string, 77
  yarn, 77
Finger Bend (action game), 170
Finger paints, 65
Finger Tips (action game), 170
First Names (word and letter game), 47
Fishing (water play game), 99
Five in a Line (checker game), 26
Flower buds, 111
Flowers, 110-11

INDEX / 187

Football (checker game), 26-27
Fox and Geese (checker game), 27
Furniture for doll house:
  curtains, 58
  match boxes, 54
  rugs, 77
  thread spools, 78-79

Games: See types of games and/or individual game titles
Garden, indoor, 112-14
Go Fish (playing card game), 40-41
Golf (ball game), 17
Gomuku (paper and pencil game), 36
Gongs, 147
Greeting cards (making), 68
Guessing (fruit game), 30
Guggenheim (word and letter game), 49

Hand push (action game), 170
Hangman (word and letter game), 47-48
Hearts (playing card game), 44
Hide and Seek (search game), 170
Hobbies, 102-07
  collections, 103
  scrapbooks, 103-07
Hot or Cold (search game), 44
House to Mouse (word and letter game), 48
Housework, 175
Hul Gul (bean game), 17

Identification games, 31
  Drop It, 31
  Feel the Raisin, 31
  Sniff, 31
  Taste It, 31
Initials (word and letter game), 48
Ink, leaf prints, 116
Inner tube arts and crafts, 76
Insects, 111-12
Invisible writing, 131-32

Jewelry:
  drinking straw, 61
  envelope, 61
  macaroni, 62
  paper, 68
  thread spool, 78
  wire, 80
Jokes, 136-39
Junk arts and crafts, 61-62
Jerk (paper game), 33-34

Key rack (making), 81
Kings (checker game), 28
Kitchen projects, 161-67
Kites (making), 107

Ladder (paper and pencil game), 37
Laugh a Little (laughter game), 31
Laundry, 97
Leaves, preserving, 114-17
  casts, 114-15
  prints, 115-17
  mounting, 117
  skeletons, 117
Letters, writing, 108-09
Lines (puzzle game), 130
Lineup (puzzle game), 125
Log cabin (making), 74
Lollipop stick arts and crafts, 62
Low Card (playing card game), 41-42

188 / INDEX

Macaroni arts and crafts:
  collage, 59
  jewelry, 62
Magazine arts and crafts, 63
Magazine games:
  Alphabet, 32
  Defacement, 59-60
  Telegrams, 32
Magic, 107
Magic Squares (number puzzle), 129
Makeup for dramatic play, 89
Maps (making), 69
Marble games:
  Bowling, 16-17
  Croquet, 45
  Roll-Away, 32
  Target, 38
Masks for dramatic play, 90
Materials and activities, 12
Memory games, 33
  California, 33
  Contents, 33
  Objects, 33
Middleman (puzzle game), 125
Mill (button game), 21-22
Missing Numbers (number puzzle), 129
Mobiles (making), 63
Model kits, 65
Morelles *see* Mill
Mounting leaves, 117
Movies (making), 54-55
Music, 146-51
  listening to, 146
  rhythm instruments (making), 147-51
  singing, 151

Nature, 110-17
  flower buds, 111
  flowers, 110-11
  insects, 111-12
  stars, 112
  indoor garden, 112-14
  preserving leaves, 114-17
Nine Men's Morris *see* Mill

Objects (memory game), 33
Odd-Even (bean game), 18

Paints, 65
Pairs (playing card game), 42
Paper arts and crafts, 65-72
  airplanes, 65-66
  canoes, 66
  chains, 67
  cut-outs, 67
  faces, 68
  greeting cards, 68
  Indian headdress, 68
  jewelry, 68
  jigsaw puzzle, 68-69
  maps, 69
  mobiles, 63-64
  parachutes, 69
  peepers, 69
  placemats, 70
  shields, 70
  snowflakes, 70
  stabiles, 64
  swish, 71
  top, 71
  weathervane, 71
  Whirligig, 71-72
Paper bag arts and crafts:
  costumes, 83-85
  dolls, 86
  hats, 87-89
  masks, 90
  puppets, 91
  village, 67
Paper bag games:
  Feel the Raisin, 31
  Toss, 23-24
Paper cup arts and crafts, 72-73
  cup-a-phone, 72-73

INDEX / 189

Paper cup games, 34-35
  Cup Stick, 34-35
  Racing Cups, 35
Paper dolls, 86
Paper games:
  chain race, 67
  Jerk, 33-34
  Target, 34
Paper and pencil games, 35-38
  Dots and Lines, 35
  Double Numbers, 35-36
  Gomuku, 36
  Ladder, 37
  Tick Tack Wheel, 37
  Triangle, 37
Paper plate arts and crafts:
  hats, 88-89
  masks, 90
  pictures, 73
Paper plate games, 38
  Quoits, 38
  Target, 38
Papier mâché, 73-74
Parachutes (making), 69
Pebble arts and crafts, 74
Peep shows (making), 54-55
Peepers (making), 69
Pen pals, 108-09
Pencil arts and crafts, 59-61
Pencil holder (making), 79
Pick Up:
  active game, 170
  drinking straw game, 30
Pictures:
  button, 56
  code writing, 132-34
  paper plate, 73
  popsicle stick, 75
Piling High (toothpick game), 46
Ping (bean game), 18
Ping-Pong balls, 16
Pipe cleaner arts and crafts, 74, 87

Pipes, bubble, 96-97
Placemats (making), 70
Playing card activities, 39
  Around the Clock, 39-40
  Go Fish, 40-41
  Hearts, 41
  Low Card, 41-42
  Pairs, 42
  Slap Jack, 42
  tents, 39
  toss, 39
  War, 42-43
Please Don't Say It! (word and letter game), 48
Popsicle stick arts and crafts, 74-75
  log cabin, 74
  pictures, 75
  rafts, 75
Potatoes:
  growing plant from, 113-14
  people, 87
  printing, 75
Printing:
  inner tube, 76
  potato, 75
  rubber sheet, 76
  stamping pad, 77
Prints, leaf, 115-17
Puppet theaters, 93-94
Puppets:
  finger, 91
  head, 91-92
  paper bag, 92
  shadow, 94-95
  sock, 92
  spoon, 92
  thumb, 92-93
Puzzles:
  Checker, 125-26
  codes, 131
  cut-out, 127
  jigsaw, 68-69
  number, 128-29

paper and pencil, 129-30
secret writing, 131-34
solutions to, 178-81
toothpick, 135
Puzzle games:
Calculations, 128
Don't Lift the Pencil, 129-30
Lines, 130
Lineup, 125
Magic Squares, 129
Middleman, 125
Missing Numbers, 129
Remove, 126
Solitaire, 126
Vice-Versa, 126

Question games, 43-44
Eleven Up, 43
Twenty Questions, 43-44
Who? Where?, 44
Quiet games, 15-50
Quoits:
clothespin game, 28
paper plate game, 38

Racing Cups (paper cup game), 35
Rafts (making), 75
Rattles, 148-49
Recipes, 161-67
Rectangle Toss (button game), 24
Release (balloon game), 16
Remove (puzzle game), 126
Riddles, 139-43
Rhythm Blocks, 149
Rhythm instruments, 147-51
Rhythm Sticks, 149
Roll-Away (marble game), 32
Roller toys (making), 55
Rubber sheet arts and crafts, 76
Rubbings (making), 59

Samplers (making), 58
Scavenger Hunt (search game), 44
Science experiments, 118-24
Air Pressure, 118-19
Balance, 119-20
Calcium, 120
Carbon Dioxide, 120-21
Crystals, 121-22
Inertia, 122-23
Magnification, 124
Sound, 124
Scrapbooks, 104-07
airplane, 104
animal, 104
astronomy, 104
baby, 104
biography, 104
car, 104-05
clothing, 105
geography, 105
government, 105
history, 105
holiday, 105
Indian, 105
interior decoration, 105
occupations, 106
ships, 106
space exploration, 106
sports, 106
train, 106
tree, 106-07
truck, 104-05
weather, 107
Sculpture:
pebble, 74
soap, 76
Search games:
Alphabet, 32
Hide and Seek, 170
Hot or Cold, 44
Scavenger Hunt, 44
Ticking Timer, 31

Secret writing, 131-34
   invisible, 131-32
   mirror, 132
   picture, 132-34
Seeds, growing plants from, 112-13
Seedlings, 113
Sentences (word and letter game), 49
Sheep and Wolves (button or counter game), 22-23
Shields (making), 70
Simon Says (action game), 170
Singing, 151
Slap Jack (playing card game), 42
Snap (button game), 23
Sniff (spice game), 30
Snowflakes (making), 70-71
Soap arts and crafts, 76
   sculpture, 76
Solitaire (puzzle game), 126
Spellbound (word and letter game), 49
Spice ball (making), 62
Stabiles (making), 64
States and Capitals (word and letter game), 49
Steeplechase (dice game), 29-30
Step Through (action game), 171
Stepping Stones (action game), 171
Stock Exchange (word and letter game), 49
Storytelling *see* Books
Strike (balloon game), 16
String arts and crafts:
   designs, 77
   musical instruments, 150
   rug for doll house, 77
   trains, 55-56

Sunshine and Rain (calendar game), 24-25
Sweet potato, growing plant from, 113
Swishes (making), 71

Target:
   paper game, 34
   paper plate game, 38
Taste It (identification game), 31
Telegrams (magazine game), 32
Tents (playing card activity), 39
Thread spool arts and crafts:
   doll, 87
   furniture for doll house, 78
   jewelry, 78
   ornaments, 78
   top, 79
   totem pole, 79
Thread spool games:
   Catch, 17
   Croquet, 45
   Toss, 45-46
Tick Tack Toe (button game), 23
Tick Tack Wheel (paper and pencil game), 37-38
Ticking Timer (kitchen timer game), 31
Tin can arts and crafts, 79
Tongue Twisters, 143-45
Toothpick arts and crafts, 79
Toothpick games:
   Dropping, 28
   Pick Up, 30
   Piling High, 46
Tops:
   bottle caps, 52
   paper, 71
   thread spool, 79

Toss:
  button game, 23-24
  calendar game, 24
  playing card activity, 39
  thread spool game, 45-46
Totem pole (making), 79
Tracings, 61
Triangle (paper and pencil game), 38
Trips *see* Excursions
Tunnels (making), 53
Twenty Questions (question game), 43-44
Twenty-Six Letters (word and letter game), 50

Vice-Versa (puzzle game), 126
Villages, making, 72
Visits *see* Excursions

War (playing card game), 42-43
Wastepaper Basket (action game), 172
Water play, 96-99
  baths, 99
  blowing bubbles, 96-97
  Fishing, 98
  laundry, 97
  Sailing, 99
Weathervanes (making), 71
Weighing (action game), 172
Whirligigs:
  button, 57
  paper, 71-72
Whittling, 81
Who? Where? (question game), 44
Wind instruments, 150-51

Wire arts and crafts, 79-80
  eyeglasses, 80
  jewelry, 80
Wood arts and crafts, 80-81
  bookends, 81
  bread board, 81
  key rack, 81
  whittling, 81
Word and letter games:
  Air, Earth, Water, 46
  Alphabet, 32
  Anagrams, 46-47
  First Names, 47
  Guggenheim, 47
  Hangman, 47-48
  House to Mouse, 48
  Initials, 48
  Please Don't Say It!, 48
  Sentences, 49
  Spellbound, 49
  States and Capitals, 49
  Stock Exchange, 49
  Telegrams, 32
  Twenty-Six Letters, 50
  Words in a Word, 50
  Wrrrrrr, 50
Words in a Word (word and letter game), 50
Writing:
  codes, 131
  invisible, 131-32
  letters, 108-09
  mirror, 132
  picture, 132-34
Wrrrrrr (word and letter game), 50
  solution to, 178

Yarn arts and crafts, 77